How to Do Successful
Business in Latin America

Your Own Guide to Exporting and Importing

D0109078

ISBN: 9781495414039

This publication is designed to provide accurate and authoritative information in regard to the subject matter covered. It is sold with the understanding that neither the author nor the publisher is engaged in rendering legal, accounting, futures securities trading or other professional service. If legal advice or other expert assistance is required, the services of a competent professional should be sought.

From the Declaration of Principles jointly adopted by a Committee of the American Bar Association and a Committee of Publishers

This book is available at special quantity discounts to use as premiums and sales promotions or for use in corporate training programs. Please call our office in Orlando, Florida at Tel. 407 - 455- 8377 for ordering. For Mr. Lopez, speaking or coaching availability visit www.AxelLopez.com or send e-mail request: info@axellopez.com

For information or to consult with Mr. Lopez for assistance in a latin american trade project, negotiation or marketing and sales support for your company, please visit: www.AmericanEMC.com

Or write to: info@AmericanEMC.com

**American Business Links, Corp.,
www.AmericanEMC.com
is an Export Management Company**

info@americanemc.com

Contents

CHAPER 7
How to Import and Sell in the
United States of America 89

CHAPTER 8
LATIN AMERICAN INFORMATION RESOURCES . . . .

Dedicated to:

To my Mom, Alex, Denise, Caesar and Evana,
thank you for your love and constant support.

To my personals friends and clients in various countries
for helping me become a citizen of the world!

About the Author
Axel G Lopez

Meet, Axel Lopez:

It is from his belief that there are two ways opportunity arrives; it can present itself by knocking on your door or you can get out there and grab it that he authored this book.

In his view either way opportunity arrives, but you definitely need to be ready when it come your way!

This book, How to Do Successful Business in Latin America, Your Own Guide to Exporting and Importing, is his contribution to helping people propel themselves beyond just thinking about success, but to take action in taking their business South of the Border and overseas!

Let me take a moment to tell you a bit more about Axel. He was born in Guatemala, Central America. While growing up in a politically turbulent area of the world, during his teenage years, in one of the worst violent times of Guatemala history he was compelled to immigrate, even, illegally to the United States.

Little did he suspect that while attempting to cross the border during his journey to the U.S. that he would be kidnapped by Mexicans at the border city with USA and he was held for ransom, his extended family living in Los Angeles paid it and he was released to an Coyote - Smuggler who sneaked him in to USA in a hidden compartment in the back of a truck.

Arriving and settling in Los Angeles, he found himself performing any type of entry level job he could find, and while working various jobs Axel studied English as a second language at night school and weekends, until he was proficient. His next goal with English knowledge was to attend College. He took the college entrance exams and was accepted and enrolled in a two year program at Los Angeles City College where he obtained a Business Associate's Degree.

Mr. Lopez was then married and chose to join the US Navy, serving a total of 5 years. He was assigned first on board USS Vancouver, a helicopter carrier ship that took them to travel to Asia for Special Military Operations during two West Pack Tours and later serving alongside the US Marines as a Field Corpsman in the desert of Kuwait and Saudi Arabia during Desert Storm/Desert Shield war.

Upon leaving the service, he received various medals and pins and an Honorable Discharge from the military. He and his family settled in Orlando, FL. Here, in the private world, he took jobs in sales in various industries before launching his own brokering business.

Mr. Lopez has 20 years of international business experience traveling around the world. He started selling medical equipment and representing other company products in Latin America. He then founded his own company, ELMED Medical Systems, Inc. (www.ElmedUSA.com) with distribution channels, sales and representation in Latin American, Middle East, Asia and European countries.

Over the years of continued traveling and business situations, Mr. Lopez, lend his Marketing and Consulting Services to individuals and companies in the international arena which prompted him to set up and begin another business. This new American company would broker, represent, translate and negotiate deals in various industries, in real estate, selling and acquiring business, construction projects, equipment, services, medical technology and has represented individual and commercial interest in various deals and negotiations in various countries.

This new business needed its own identity and organization to offer his services as an International Business Marketing Consulting and Sales company, and now operates as, American Business Links, Corp. based in Orlando, FL.

American Business Links, Corp., (www.AmericanEMC.com) is an Export Managing Company that primarily focuses on business consulting, representations, distribution, business matching, marketing, speaking and assist with international contract negotiations on behalf of American, European, South American and Middle Eastern companies.

Mr. Lopez is in active member, and volunteer, of the Hispanic Business Initiative Fund, Hispanic and International Chambers of Commerce, the International Round-Table and actively participates and attends International Business Networking events and Latin American business functions, including traveling in U.S. government sponsored Trade Missions to Latin America on behalf of his clients.

Mr. Lopez has two well-educated and successful children, Denise and Caesar, both of whom are corporate attorneys in CT and NY. He lives with wife Evana in Orlando, FL. Mr. Lopez holds a Bachelor's Degree in Business and Marketing from Columbia College.

He takes great pride in events that have made the most difference to in his life, these include;

- Being born and has lived in a foreign country

- His US Navy military service life and experience

- Traveling extensively worldwide and visiting most USA cities on business

- His ongoing self-education, attending business events, reading books and Networking!

The goal for Mr. Lopez's work on this book is clear; it is to inspire you, the reader!

"Most of us live an abundant life full of opportunities, left and right. And as the saying goes, if you cannot find them, MAKE them!"

When asked how the subject of this book relates to his life, his answer was simple and direct, "When I first began seeking to do business in these markets, I did not have any contacts or was not aware of any sources of information or tools that could help me succeed in the region, so it took a lot of travel, trails and errors and many business trips to learn to master international trade. Through this book, I will share my experiences and provide you with critical guidance and knowledge that you can implement it to your own business and succeed".

The good news from Latin America, from my own experience, is a great place to do business.

So, let's get started, now!

Introduction

Why do Business in Latin America

In case you are not aware of, a diverse consumer market of more than 550 million people live in Latin America!

These people, we call Latinos, live, work and spend money, just south of the U.S. Border! However, I am not talking about Mexico, although is included, but there are many other countries, territories, islands and protectorates in the Latin American Region that await for your business.

Within this huge market, there is hunger and demand for American and Foreign goods, technology, know-how and services.

You might know the existence of plenty multilateral and bilateral free-trade agreements between U.S. and many Latin American countries, that are designed to offer your business a competitive edge over other European and Asian rivals. These trade agreements should propel you to enter or expand your business in Latin American. You need to know, that Free trade agreements help you compete on prices, quality, as well as offering prompt delivery of your goods and services to these markets.

I have witnessed over my 20 years of traveling to the region, how U.S. technology, management, know-how, goods, and services from a wide range of industries have contributed significantly to the growth of Latin American economies.

Countries like Mexico, Chile, Colombia, Brazil and Costa Rica, no name a few, actively solicit foreign trade investments from American companies. Another benefit to these trade agreements is consumer and industrial products find their way to markets and many factories are settled in Latin America to promote business and employment opportunities. Many countries of Latin America, now, enjoy political, government and economic stability.

I want to emphasize that you can view the Latin American market as a conglomeration of markets, people, language, religions, economy, laws, cultures, and currencies…that all may seem similar, but each country is very unique and different to deal with. You have been adviced.

Here is a list of the *most known* countries that make up the Latin America region:

Antigua and Barbuda	Guyana
Argentina	Haiti
The Bahamas	Honduras
Barbados	Jamaica
Belize	Nicaragua
Bolivia	Mexico
Brazil	Panama
Cuba	Paraguay
Chile	Peru
Colombia	Puerto Rico
Costa Rica	Saint Kitts and Nevis
Dominica	Saint Lucia
Dominican Republic	Saint Vincent and the Grenadines
Ecuador	Suriname
El Salvador	Uruguay
Grenada	Trinidad and Tobago
Guatemala	Venezuela

As you can appreciate, as a whole the Latin America Region is one, but each country is independent and separate from one to another. The region is an Emerging Market in terms of economic conditions and buying power. Because of its natural resources and thriving markets, many countries and businesses and individual investors are seeking the Latin America region for new business. Many of these countries have been ignored due to economic, social or political reasons in the past, but the economic conditions of today are better and the demand for goods and services has increased over the years and it will continues rising in this region.

In general all Latin American nations are now moving toward having a place in the global economy. We have to realize that most of its citizens in these countries are no longer under military rule, and only a handful of them have state-controlled economies or unworkable democratic administrations. Over the last decades, most of these countries have shifted to establishing changes in political institutions of power and democratic capitalistic leadership, many countries have improved financial systems, and many have developed environmental and social awareness which has helped them to develop and get on the international business trade arena by creating new products and services in exchange for demanding more from foreign sources.

Let me introduce you to this emerging region and welcome you to:
How to Do Successful Business in Latin America!

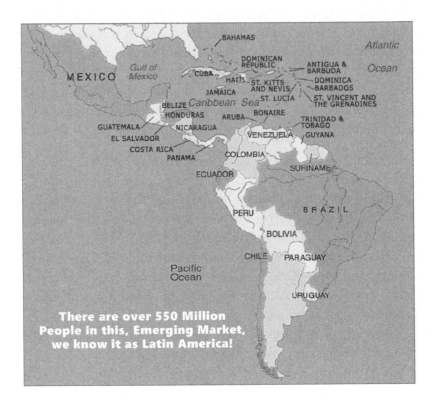

An Emerging New Latin - American Region

Let me state it, one more time, Latin America is not a country or a single market, it's a region!

There are many independent countries, territories, islands, commonwealths, and protectorates with more than 550 million people who speak hundreds of dialects, originating from Spanish, Portuguese, French, German, Dutch, Italian, Creole, and native Amerindian tongues, that make this Emerging Market region. However, the most known Latin American countries are to be around 25 independent countries but there are more!

Each country is unique, and even inside their own countries, some areas have economic differences and development, social conditions and political environments, as well as a variety of other factors that should alert you that a separate strategic marketing plan must be devised for each country when you intend to target and do business in the region.

When doing business in Latin America, planning of course is necessary. You must define your strategy to break in the country of your choosing, especially if you plan to invest in setting up an assembly or production plant, distribution centers, or customer-service facilities where you will be dealing with local laws, government rules and political interests. However you are not alone, for your information, there are thousands of foreign companies doing business in the region for years, many for even decades, that have been able to achieve success the same way you can being prepared and knowing where, how, who and when to enter a particular market.

If we revisit the history of the region, over the past 500 years, Latin America has been alternately conquered by foreign mercenaries, exploited by powerful foreign companies, occupied by military foreign troops, immersed in civil wars that have been funded and supported by foreign governments, and pounded by hurricanes, droughts, earthquakes, and volcanic eruptions and surprisingly, all in all, after so many years of tumultuous changes, Latin America shines with business opportunities to investors and companies, who wants to do business there.

Economically, politically and historically, the 'real mother country', Spain, as is known to the majority of Spanish speaking people in countries and islands in Latin America, abandoned control of this vast region and allowed other countries, primarily the United States to come in to the rescue with economic and political influences. To many countries in the region, the U.S.A. is like a foster parent to most governments influencing and establishing control thus promoting capitalism.

In general, Latin America is reluctant to traditional American marketing, production, personnel policies and the ways of doing business, but this continues to change, I recommend that you learn, understand, adjust and adapt your marketing approach to enter these markets their own way not yours. Keep in mind that most deals, projects and negotiations take place because of 'relationships', yes, I am not talking about family relationships only. As we will cover later in this book, most 'business relationships' take time to establish you need to be properly introduced or blessed by someone to gain their trust. Business relationships in many instances depending on the product or service you represent will take time to solidify and convert to business, I will then remind you, do not rush, be patient.

I cannot emphasize enough just how important it is for you to research the country where you are most interested in doing business with and become knowledgeable of various of its factors and conditions. The more knowledge, data and research, the better prepared you will be to close a deal, find a representative or distributor or perhaps setting up your own business inside the country of your choosing, if that makes sense to your business and bottom line.

As you study more this great business region, you will find yourself immersed in dealing with various cultures, attitudes, and beliefs. Among, the things you ought to know and understand include:

- The history of the country and government
- Language
- Religion
- Holidays
- Major cultural events
- Its famous traditions and holidays
- Gift exchanging
- The politics of the country
- The traditional role of women
- Uncommon laws and protection
- Famous cultural heroes
- Education and people culture
- The role of family and relationships
- Currency and Money exchange
- Food
- Etiquette
- Salutations and Greetings
- Business agreements and commitments
- Security

Of course this is a partial list but in the chapters ahead, we will see the significance of this knowledge and how they can affect your business. What I recommend is you take your list with you, and do two things with it; learn it and live it and apply it in building your own business relationships.

You can learn about everything on this list from public and college libraries, the Internet, U.S. Government materials, and from the country itself. Visiting the country or living in it may pose a greater challenge initially, but when appropriate it can be done. Before embarking in business or going to a country, check out business clubs, associations, organizations, or even friends or relatives might be familiar with the country. Spend time and talk to the folks of a given country, let them know what you are up to and likely they will give you good pointers for you to get started.

Who is this book for?

How to do Successful Business in Latin America is a guide for the person or company who wishes to profit from international trade in the region.

You the owner of a business that manufactures, sells and distributes or assembles a product or sells a service. You, the person, who is looking for an international career. You, an entrepreneur who wants to tap in to a purchasing power of an emerging market of more than 550 Million people and may be lacking hands on experience on international trade or you that only wants to learn the mechanics of exporting or importing in Latin America.

Personally, I have achieved most of my experience by traveling directly to the region and dealing directly with the private and government sector, for years, and putting in practice practical know-how information, building business relationships, approaching government officials, visiting with the international business community in most countries and dealing directly with distributors, agents and key business people, all the while representing the business interests of American and Foreign companies.

The Latin America represent in many sectors an untapped business opportunity for the private and government sectors that can change your life and business, so wait not more, get into the export and import business now.

CHAPTER 1
What is Latin American Trade?

The international trade business is the exchange of goods and services across borders.

As an example, most clothing that we wear is now sewn in member countries of the Dominican Republic and Central American Free Trade region (DR-CAFTA). Offshore call centers are set up and managed from Jamaica, Costa Rica, or Barbados. Aside from Ecuador, Colombian flowers dominate the bulk of the U.S. market. Chilean and Argentinean wines are served in many restaurants. Mexican vegetables, Honduran fruit, Guatemalan coffee, and many other crops and products made or assembled in Mexico, Colombia, Costa Rica have made their way in U.S. markets in exchange for many countless services, know how, products and technology from North America, Europe or Asia.

Let's define the two activities that make Latin America trade possible, exports and imports:

Exports are the goods and services we sell to other nations. As example, an American Company, sell its products or services to a Brazilian company. This company will be shipping and exporting to Brazil. These products or services will be sold, used or consumed in Brazil.

Imports are the goods and services nations purchase and consume in country. Example, an American company who buys the goods and or services from Brazilian companies to be sold, used or consumed in America, means that the American company will be importing from Brazil.

Over these past 2 decades, major changes in information exchange, the internet, traveling options, bigger ports, transportation and governments have ease many countries restrictions and even limitations to doing imports and exports. There is a great demand from consumers that need or want products and services from other nations who are willing to pay the price, not matter what that price is for quality, recognition or their likes. If they have the money consumers will find a way to pay and get what they want from you!

Understand that many companies because of their size, lack of experienced trade personnel, may end up outsourcing their export or import functions to individual agents or hiring an Export Managing Companies (EMCs) who are more familiar with the trade process.

If you know this emerging market called Latin America, and you own a business or work independently, this could be a great business opportunity for you as well. As I see it, many companies and consumers may benefit from your 'know how' in getting products or services from key suppliers.

Latin trade can offer you the opportunity to act on behalf of a company or buyer, as an International middleman, who sells, represents or distribute a product or service for export or import, as I have been able to do for years with my company, American Business Links, Corp. and so can you applying your knowledge.

Understanding Latin America Culture, Region and People

It is important that you get to know the following, most Latin America governments have made progress with their economic reforms but poverty levels and income inequalities are pronounced in some areas. If you are visiting a particular country those facts will be clear from the moment of your arrival, you will notice two sides in society in many countries, the people that have, and the ones that have noting, and is easy distinguished.

While many Latin American countries have become less risky to invest and do business, it should be obvious that doing business in any Latin American country is not always easy not matter what product or service you offer or how to meet the demand of the country. You must learn early on where is it you are going and have someone, preferably an in-country person with contacts, to guide you as to what is what and who is who before entering the market, this approach can lead you to do business right away.

Realize that most people in these countries will proclaim an eagerness and willingness, for international investment and trade, but the reality is that things move at a different or slower pace than in USA or Europe, when it comes to foreign trade and business transactions.

I started traveling on business in Latin America in the early 90's and I had to quickly get myself trained and adapted to dealing with local folks and started to understand our different cultures and similarities. Based on my experience, when you pursue business in this region, forget the "American Way" or for that matter the Foreign Way of conducting and doing business. In Latin America there is only the "Latino Way", which we will cover later, but for now I will suggest that wherever you go or whoever you are meeting with, you do not jumping right into a business situation right away but get the chance to learn and build relationships. When you deal with Latin American people, learn to pace yourself, warm up, chit-chat, adjust your tone, show courtesy while showing professionalism and respect, your host will appreciate that and you will get their trust in return that will form the foundation of a successful business relationship.

We must become sensitive to understand local custom, learn something about each country, diversity, differences, timing and courtesies to avoid conflicts and misunderstandings. And remember when you travel to the region, we are guests in their country, and as the good old saying goes: "When in Rome, Do as the Romans Do".

Some of the following traits of Latin American peoples' mentality you need to keep in mind when doing business are the following:

- Observe and respect for Age and Experience

- Most People display a Happy and Easy Going, No Rush Life Style and Let Live Attitude

- Relationships, Family values and Interest Recognition

- Income, Race, Names and Class Separation

- Politics and the Power of the Church and Religious Beliefs

Observe and Respect for Age and Experience

When possible, use senior marketing and business development personnel to negotiate orders or contracts. Latin American and Caribbean business people, in general, trust doing business with senior people in age or company seniors in position or titles, as that you will be considered and believed "as being serious", trustworthy and experienced.

Age demands a degree of respect in many countries. Age or Seniority implies wisdom and experience to most people in Latin America. I will advice that young executives should make the initial contacts with business owners, bureaucrats, potential sales representatives, agents, distributors and buyers, if necessary but senior people or high ranking company officers should close the deal.

In Latin America, when dealing with a customer, supplier, or government official who is clearly your elder, restrain your impatience, be courteous and have respect for that person's age, title or position, if you want their attention and get a business closed.

Latin America Easy-Going No Rush Lifestyle

When you visit Latin America you will notice that life moves at slower pace in Latin America than in most American States or even European countries. Nonetheless, metropolitan cities, like Bogota, Sao Pablo, Mexico City, Lima, Caracas, Santiago and even San Jose are jammed with traffic because of extended rushed hours, antiquated roads or limited transportation options makes moving around very slow.

Do not be a surprise that you might be the only one rushing to go places when you are in Latin America. I have come to accept and believe that slower or limited modes of transportation and lack of roads and infrastructure, warmer weather tend to slow the pace of everyday life. This slower, no rush-relaxed lifestyle, plus the natural Latin affinity for leisure pursuits, extended breaks, meals, social and family activities, holidays and bureaucratic government processes leads to a laid back attitude about virtually everything, including doing business.

When we compare that lifestyle situation to the American Way of doing business, we tend to move quickly, get the job done, close the order, and get on our way to the next meeting or appointment, almost any obstacle that slows us down becomes an irritant and we need to remove it quickly as soon as possible and get to the order. After all, we have deadlines to meet, commitments to fulfill and planes to catch. We set a time for a meeting or appointment and expect other parties to be there on time. If the meeting is supposed to end at noon, we expect it to end at noon so we can make our luncheon appointment and continue about our business. This is not the case things are done in many countries in Latin America.

In America business life, normally, we don't have time to exchange pleasantries, chit-chat and smell the aroma of coffee or the flowers, we want the business first then we will have time for that when we retire. However, if you take this approach while doing business in Latin American countries, I guarantee, you will not get the job done in coming to an agreement or closing the deal. It will not happen, the social and business pace is different and you will need to adjust your speed and tempo in doing business in the region.

I have experienced this many times in person, and I have witnessed firsthand, when exposed to foreign executives meetings how they fail or succeed. Mostly what makes the difference in business meetings is not going too fast on your presentations or showing how much you know about your product or service but by taking a breath, talking commonalities and the small chit chat, talking about current events before engaging in business that makes an impression. Let your host lead the conversations or your presentation, they will tell you when they want to start to hear you, where, how, and who they want in their meetings, follow their lead, if you want to be successful.

In almost all Latin American countries, business dealings are based on personal, one-on-one relationships. We, Latinos, from the time you arrive, we want to get to know you, from where you are from to how is your family, your children, your story, how was your trip, hotel, and usually you will get offered something, or if you need anything while you are visiting that it can be provided to you to make your visit a good one. Many people want to hear from you, what is your opinion about their country and why you are there?

Latinos expect you to have an interest, opinion or your interpretation of events occurring in their country or past history, as a means of establishing commonality with you, as this is their way of life. Most people at any social economic status keep up with daily, current local events and international news affecting their country from newspapers, magazines, the radio and television sets.

In general, Latinos, are very proud people not matter what their circumstances and economic status is, they will defend their ground. This pride begins with a strong nationalistic bias acquired from its ancestors, tradition or heritage, regardless of the difficulties their countries may have encountered in the past or are experiencing at a time. While having said that, a word of caution, restrain your views on political opinions and religious points of view when talking in social events or in a formal business settings or meetings, as you might be out casted from your own comments or biased observations. Keep it to yourself!

When dealing with Latinos, you will witness this laid-back attitude, that essentially runs at all levels of society, in private and government circles, it absorbs at times an excessive amount of time before getting to real business but that is the way it is in most regions and most people. If you are not willing to ignore the clock like the rest of Latin Americans, you shouldn't do business in this region.

Believe it or not, contrary to what we are used to believe, to succeed in this region, you must be ready and willing to move slowly, learn to go with the flow rather than to push forward to quick conclusions or rushing in. But in moving slow, I mean, ensure you are talking to the right business or government connected people to get you the business you are seeking.

This 'go with the flow timing' is true whether you are visiting, making a presentation, marketing, negotiating a contract, selling a product, handling customer complaints, or dealing with government officials, exercise courtesy, patience, maturity and professionalism.

Relationships, Family Values and Interests

Most Latinos prefer to live their personal lives as if there is no tomorrow. To describe this means to "Live for Today, because, Tomorrow we do not know what is going to happen". But where this attitude comes from? It is my research and opinion that decades of turmoil and instability in Latin America countries have affected most economies due to changes in government leaderships, military influence and control, or natural disasters that affect their very own way of life and economy.

So I tend to agree with some research found that most Latino people do spend a lot today, because their money may lose its value tomorrow due to inflation. Savings or investing is not generally done due to uncertainty of government intervention or political changes and even due to international news that may affect their economy. I have seen it and has heard it, most Latinos believe and have a free spirited opinion full of optimism and hopes that things will be Ok, that things will get better tomorrow, but for now, live it today.

A strong Latin America virtue, as a Latino, is that families have a strong bond for the family well being, not matter what. Regardless of their social class, there is a tremendous amount of closeness between family, extended family and friends. When you deal with Latinos you will witness, from the business stand point, how the people you engage usually will consult a family member or childhood classmate or a close friend of their relative for opinion that will influence a decision to do business with you.

Therefore, knowing that relationships are critical in business dealings, you must know, Who knows Who, to get things done!

On this subject, being aware of who you are dealing with and who these people consult with locally will make your business efforts simpler, shorter and more productive. Not everyone you meet wants something in return, although opinions and influence comes with a price many times, depending on what is at stake, it is interesting to see how much the opinion of an experienced elder or someone in a key position, someone with a family name or social class, influences a business deal, not matter if the business is at private or government level, it will affect a negotiation or an agreement.

Any local key opinion leader will point to you who the customers, clients, suppliers, bureaucrats and business partners are to get a project or negotiation closed. This means, depending on your business objectives, time and resources, in building these critical business relationships you might end up mingling and attending government functions, social and sports events, church activities, graduation or even wedding ceremonies. Whatever it takes, do it. Latinos expect you to be involved, you become part of their extended family, these relationships helps you meeting more people, that eventually will help you overcoming the regulations that most countries imposes to foreigners or closing a deal.

Income, Race, Heritage, Origin, Education and Class Separation

Racial standing and mix varies from country to country depending on the people's country of origin, as most people have come from: Spain, Italian, German, French, English, Portuguese, or Dutch roots.

In most Latin American countries, the top class ranking is 'white Spanish' first, in the case of Brazil 'white Portuguese', this class is followed by the mix races, called Mestizos/Creoles/Ladinos, then the indigenous Amerindians and the Afro-American descendents.

In the majority of these groups not matter where, socio economic class standing, wealth and family name heritage is very important, if you are doing business with the elite class that might control industries or business sectors is better you must be recommended or allow someone to introduce you, as is some societies, these are a very closed group.

While the majority of countries in Latin America are controlled by Spanish or European descendents, in the West Indian Caribbean states are the exception, where top government and business positions are held by Blacks with many British influence, laws and culture and some Whites. In West Indian cultures, race is less important, but wealth and family heritage has a lot of weight in business relationships.

Another consideration is that women have made inroads in the business community and top government positions, including Presidents of Countries as the case of Chile, Brazil, Costa Rica, Panama, Nicaragua, however, the traditional legendary 'Macho Man' is very evident in all society circles, in most countries, cities and regions. For years, males have standards of behavior and expectations that are substantially different from females as the bread winners.

Of course times have passed and living conditions, in metropolitan cities, many hard working women are the breadwinners and many hold leadership positions in the private and government sector, but do recognize early in negotiations who wears the pants, so to speak, when it comes to business decision making.

There are a lot of females in charge, in private and government, who consult a senior for approval to take decisions and commitments, learn to recognize early who takes the final decisions while negotiating. We must be aware also that a more visible, louder, and more demanding male voice, does not mean, that things will get done, seek the women in charge!

Just a note to female professionals, engaging in traveling and doing business in Latin America, behave and dressed professionally! Everyone loves to host and do business with foreigners, but males tend to love foreign women more. So it is not uncommon that they will display affection and interest so behave accordingly, show them you can have a good time, and that you can get the business closed.

It is my belief and assumption in traveling, studying and dealing with Latin American people that racial bias is inherited from the Spanish Conquistadores background. The general attitude is: 'I am better than you because we came from European roots'. And, also, because of the struggles for political powers, social control, and economic events experienced over the years. Those who have a particular last name, or came from a particular European country or Middle Eastern region, or the children of these families who went to school at a well renown local or international private school continues to exercise control in many industries or hold political power in many of these countries.

Racial bias, as in U.S.A. or some European countries, manifests itself in several ways, from the differences in skin color to cultural heritage of each individual or even the region in their own country where people live. In Latin American, people tend to judge one to another, on buying and selling or doing business with based on those differences. All assumptions are based on peoples' Education, place of Origin, Race, Heritage or Wealth of the Family.

I can only encourage you and suggest that before you go out there to offer your products and services, first get to know the people you will be dealing with to make your business negotiations faster, by identifying who is who. Although at the private level things go faster than the government business do, I encourage you to learn who you are dealing with, and who do they do business or talk to, before they do business with you. Be alert!

Politics and the Power of the Church / Religion

Regardless of your religious and political views, the following are just some well known facts, documented history and things that I have witnessed and experienced over my many years of ongoing traveling to major metropolitan and rural areas of many countries in Latin America.

Let's begin with some history, in efforts from major European powers for conquest, resources, discoveries, gold and gain territory expansion, Spain, Portugal, English, Italian and French sent their armies to take claims on New Found Territories and Islands. The Spanish crown, sent many missionaries along their conquering armies to help convert this Ameri-Indians to follow and bow to the powers of "Mother Land" Spain.

While it is a known fact that most indigenous civilizations in Latin America and the Caribbean predated those of European people, the Conquistadores and the Church missioners put forth their superiority and powers instilling fears to all of these indigenous people. These indigenous people were considered by the Spanish as uncultured, naked, pagans that had to be converted one way or another and be put to their service and slavery, alongside the Afro-Americans brought by them from Africa.

You must visit the countries where Incas, Arawak and Mayan people lived and you will see the signs of terror that was descendent over these people to have their own sacred beliefs, rituals, places of worship and customs changed. The Conquistadores imposed a new system and a belief system of a Supreme Being that everyone had to abide by, or suffer the consequences of slavery, torture or death.

Jesuit priests and conquering armies taught and enforce that the authority of a 'Supreme Being' overshadowed that of their own Gods or local government and customs. In order to succeed this indoctrination they were punished hard, and subjected the Indians as they did Afro-American blacks to slavery, tortures and killings.

The acts committed to Ameri-Indian population are all unimaginable atrocities and violence. These indigenous people has gone through this abuse also in North America, U.S.A. and other continents like Australia and Africa, but at the end the oppressors converted most of these Ameri-Indians beliefs to adopt a New faith, and to praised a new God. Not choice was given to the original American Indian population but to live in fear and do as the Spanish ordered or they would pay the consequences. The Spanish got their way from these people, obedience, servitude and their lands.

This type of indoctrination mandated by any means necessary to include Fear of the devil, Fear of fire, Fear of challenging authority and Fear of going to hell. And to obtain Salvation they better followed the Church, the power and authority of whoever was in charge. You might think, that Almighty was in favor not with the Indians but with the conquistadores and priests, as divine representatives that allow them special powers and rule over the rest of the people.

As I continue traveling to the region, I cannot help to reflect, and ponder on how those practices, although now more subtle, continue after all of these years, not with forced tortures, punishments and death but forced beliefs that 'our God' is better than their own ancestral beliefs and that at any socio economic level you will encounter those beliefs fully engrained.

Up to this date in a number of countries, capital cities and rural areas, the evidence is clear of how these missionaries and armies forced the Church and the belief of a Higher Power over the beliefs of the indigenous people. Wherever you go, you will see the amount of Churches spread over their land. Most of these buildings still exist in central parks and plazas, you will see the power of the Church building standing next to the Presidential, Governors or Mayor's palace. As in the past years, still holds true now, the influence of religious beliefs, peoples obedience and respect for higher authority has been shaped by the Church.

If you translated these beliefs into daily life, this eternal search for salvation has given many people, including the poor, non believers and pagan people hope for a better tomorrow. Their message still loud continues for a glorious hereafter. Pentecostal preachers teach the need to obey spiritual authority and to docilely accept the often cruel, abusive, limited and inhumane conditions of this life. What I see, personally, is that no one really cares but to look out for your salvation.

Religious as racial prejudice exist, just as it has existed in U.S. or by European countries, although most people are mestizos, that is of mixed race between indigenous Amerindian and Spanish (as an example), still you have the difference or where you came from, heritage, or wealth. Of course, less racial bias exist in the private business community, but is evident to see who makes more money, holds key positions, gets opportunities, holds government positions and in many cities who owns or what groups of people control industries and monopolies.

When you are visiting Latin American countries, recognize the existence of racial bias, religious, education, heritage, wealth and gender, you will not be able to do much about it, but be alert when dealing with bureaucrats, the military, customs and other authority figures, in private as well as government people, and keep your opinions to what it is and what is not, to yourself.

Keep in mind that you are in the region for business, not to change racial injustices or beliefs, let the locals manage their own business. In favoring racially oppressed groups or stop injustices in an attempt to right a national wrong you might lose track of your business purpose and the people you are dealing with may fire back at you and not get the business.

I will suggest that maintaining a middle of the road policy, restraining opinions on how things are in U.S.A. or other European countries is a sensible solution and is better to stick to a business agenda, after all, that is the reason you went there to begin with.

It is wise to have Political and Religious views, opinions, discussions out of the negotiation table and in social settings, as always in your regular meetings and traveling someone is there to watch, hear and judge your professionalism, your attitude and your willingness to do business with them. So stick to business!

Learn Latin American Culture

The international business person should be aware that culture differs from one country to another. Even people within its own country may act and behave differently from one area to another, as culture is composed of languages, religion, origin, heritage, values, attitudes, laws, education, politics, economic and social organizations.

Many years ago, I do not give accountability of day in today's modern days, but Japanese people before penetrating a foreign market, companies send their managers to live and study to chosen country. Their mission was to develop relationships that will last for years to come. They were not there looking to change the way of life of the host country people, but to learn to live, adjust and accept situation and circumstances, as is was. When those folks achieved the knowledge they wanted, they went back to their company and brought with them their mighty marketing and production capabilities and unload them on the host country. In most recent years, in my travels, I see this strategy applied by the Chinese now in many businesses and industries, essentially worldwide.

In developing overseas alliances with the challenges of distance, dealing with different cultural motivations and priorities represent elements of risk, rewards and due diligence. The best way to appreciate another culture is to "walk in the other person's shoes" to feel for the similarities and differences. When you learn these things of behavior you can adjust and direct your marketing efforts to capitalize on business opportunities.

When you travel, as example from U.S.A. to any other Latin American country, avoid culturally sensitive language, jokes or expressions that may offend your host. The American media is saturated with great advertising campaigns to promote a product or service that when viewed by other countries, it does not make any sense whatsoever.

If you are developing media campaigns, hire the services of local media players to convey the message of your product according to their own way of advertising. Catchy words, slang and phrases, normally, do not work or can translate to an entirely different meaning when translated to Spanish or Portuguese.

When you develop a marketing and promotional campaign that involves copy in advertising ensure the meaning is understood correctly by the customers you are trying to reach. While everyone, except Brazil, speaks Spanish, the same words may have a different meaning in Mexico, Argentina, Colombia or Guatemala.

Many of the words, expressions and depending on the people you deal with in certain countries or regions, will speak in double meanings, a jargon that gives many words sexual innuendo that come from a heavy influence and mixes of European languages and Spanish.

For instance in the U.S.A. one of the cars by Chevrolet that was a bestseller some years ago was called, Nova, and not one executive in Detroit could figure out why this vehicle was not selling much in neighboring Mexico, a country that for years buys lots of American made vehicles, the problem was not the car, mileage per gallon, the interior, the quality of its sound system, warranty, design or amount of seats, but it was its name, Nova. When you translate it to Spanish, it means Not Go! Who wants pay premium dollars for a car that does 'not go'?

Another situation is the simple word *coger*, it means to hold on, in Mexico or Colombia, but depending on how it is said and to who and in what a particular situation, it will describe getting in a sexual act, as that is the way it will be interpreted in Argentina or Dominican Republic. The word *bicho* that refers to insects in Mexico, in Puerto Rico, it gets interpreted to a man's penis. The same is true with words like *pan* to most of us just means bread, but to some other countries the interpretation may be referring to women's vigina. In a recent visit to Central America, I saw a company campaign, with its head-line, *Desfrijolizece!* a made up word, a combination of slang meant to translate to the reader to 'eat not beans, anymore' when in reality what they want to convey is that people ought to afford other things other than what they usually are used to and be able to afford the advertised product. This kind of thing only confuses potential consumers, there is too much room for different meanings and interpretations. It might be clever but not effective. Some people in reading it can take offense on how dare they tell me not to eat what they love to eat, too many folks eat beans as part of the regular diet or custom. Other people can wonder very far from the advertiser intended message.

Along these lines, the only way to avoid making a very serious error in your advertising copy, product or service description is to hire a translator from the country in which you intent to do business. It only makes sense to be sure that your message says what you really mean it to say. No one intentionally wants to offend customers but do recognize that many words and phrases commonly used in our country and language may have an entirely different, or even offensive meanings in a Latin America country.

If you are using pictures, photos, symbols and colors in your company product or service literature material, be alert about the use and the meaning of its colors. Red, purple, orange, black, and so on may not have any important meaning in the American culture, but they may be offensive in Latin societies or targeted customer group. It Brazil, for example, the color purple is usually interpreted as the color of death and in other place it relates to holy week and religious celebrations in Guatemala or Mexico, so do not use unless you are selling products or services related to that color.

If you are a foreign company, ensure you consult locally about language, customs, use of colors, review statements that may have double meaning or brand names, symbols or markings that may be offensive or be taken out of context. I will advice to consult with local experts.

Dealing with Latin American Political and Economic Environment

Your Latin American market strategy must be medium to long term to be effective. It doesn't make much sense to invest money and time in a country that is politically unstable or has a shaky economic future. As stated before, most of your business negotiations will happen once you have developed and established good business relationships.

It's prudent to do get some basic country assessment of the local market to determine if the market is accessible to your products or services and that over a reasonably period of time it will be steady and increase profitability to your company. Of course, no one has a crystal ball to predict the future as things can change politically and economically. Therefore putting together as many specific facts and opinions as possible regarding the chosen market, your local business partner representation and capability will help you reduce the risk of unrealistic growth projections.

There are many international trade periodicals and journals, and some U.S. government agencies and State agencies whose focus is on promoting trade and foreign investment, some of which provide excellent coverage of Latin America, the most reliable and current information about political and economic conditions will come from the host-country offices of the American Chamber of Commerce, multinational banks, multinational accounting and consulting firms, and in-country subsidiaries or divisions of other American companies that may share their own insights of the local market.

The following questions should be asked of representatives from each organization to check out economic and political environment:

- What does the country's main economic base consist of? Imports? Exports?

- What are some of the locally produced goods and services?

- Are statistics available to show economic growth or decline (for example, gross domestic product, interest rates, inflation rates, annual capital expenditures, imports, exports, wage rates, unemployment rates)? If so, what are they, and how reliable are they?

- What are the country's demographic trends (for example, age spread, income distribution, geographic dispersion, and so on)?

- Are major businesses owned or controlled by the government?

- Are there any privatization programs under way and how many major businesses being sold?

- How strong are local business cartels or what monopolies exist?

- What specific trade barriers block foreign imports or foreign investment? Licensing? Exchange controls? Protected industries?

- Do government regulations restrict the distribution of imported products?

The answers to some of those critical questions ought to give you a panoramic view of the local market opportunities, limitations, size of market before option to invest in pursuing business in the chosen territory for your products or services.

Poverty and Crime in Latin America and Business Opportunities

Some studies suggest that one of the reasons why some Latin American countries are considered violent is because poverty has increased amongs its peopleb, opportunities are limited, corruption is rampant and social inequalities exist bluntly. There is no surprised that the most marginalized groups are the Indian, Afro-descendants, women and children.

This situation then begs the question then, Why any individual, American or Foreign company should enter or seek Latin American markets as long as these conditions prevails, crimes and criminals operate openly and governments seem unable or unwilling to protect their own citizens?

On the surface, and quick answer is: No one should. However, hundreds of companies are very active in Latin America and more are entering every year, the reasoning in the market place is because, 'if there are problems there, a need or want also exist for your products and services'.

For instance, if you sell products and services, like security systems, surveillance technology, tracking software, security services, protected vehicles, you have found yourself thriving markets. If you have initiatives to relocate, assembly, expand or manufacture you found yourself an available and great labor reliable pool selection and incentives to get your company settled. If your products or services are in the education arena, or your company offers financing, programs that help children and women, nutritional products, food or beverages for women and families. My dear reader, you have great markets to explore and capitalize on.

By stating those examples, is not to say, that all, these region is unsafe, violent, criminal or unjust, as those things do occur in every corner of world and around every local town or city in U.S., however, I do advice use common sense and see how your product or service fills a need or want in a private sector and government level and go get the business.

CHAPTER 2

Where do you start:
Country Search and Business Survey of Latin America

It makes sense to start making market research before you venture in to Latin American markets. The demand for your product or service should be an indicator to allow you to invest time, money and resources to find out the potential growth of market. This research should produce enough data to make intelligent marketing, financial, manufacturing, licensing, or distribution decisions for your company.

This research is critical, if you are looking to investing or in forming a new in-country business. You will be able to calculate a business strategy and assess country and business risk. The more information you gather and apply to your business, you will be able to avoid costly mistakes.

Whenever possible, I normally consult for up to date information using available government resources like the U.S. Commercial Service, International Chambers of Commerce, American in Country Chambers of Commerce and by attending international business networking events that offer reliable political, social and economic data, as well as market and industry specific information.

If you reside in the U.S.A. the U.S. Commercial Service can help you and your business to do some leg work providing you with extensive and comprehensive data relating to your product or service and analyze its pros and cons of entering a particular Latin American market. The Commercial Service assistance is very reliable and affordable and it does not require you to travel there to gather this information, most embassies offer this service too for their own country trade interest.

While several U.S. government agencies and Latin trade chambers, news, periodicals will give you a fairly good feel for current political and economic events, experience has shown me that to get the full appreciation of the business venture, once you have gathered some reliable information, you need to see for yourself, that means visiting Latin American country markets, yes, it means: You traveling to the country.

When you visit Latin America, you ought to identify the following information for your business:

- Who might be the Resellers-Wholesalers or Distribution channels

- Agents and Sales representatives

- Media and Advertising available

- In-Country Regulations, Trade Compliance requirements, legal aspects of the business

- What is the business conditions in country, tax incentives, money exchanges, banking and payment regulations

- Economy and Political Stability

All the above answers is critical to learn, if one of your objectives of your business happens to be establishing a local assembly or manufacturing operation, distribution, or even openning an office, you will also need information about real estate, buildings or office space, hiring practices, hiring labor, transportation, materials and supplies, legal and accounting professional advice support.

As you can appreciate, it is better when you are able to gather all pertinent information ahead or see it for yourself, and also, there is a much better cost effective proposition by hiring the services of an expert international consultant or firm or hire an outside Export Management Company to render professional counsel and advice on international business and marketing.

If you elect to hire outside International Consulting services, follow theses suggested guidelines:

1. Define your objectives, what do you want your Consultant to do for you and to recommend you the best strategy to enter the market

2. Give the consultant all related information about your company, products or services, where are you currently doing business, business capabilities and your personnel staff support, commitment and knowledge and availability to service the market.

3. Learn from your Consultant, how they operate and what research methodology they plan to use, costs, time, resources, travels, etc.

4. If your company has already business leads, information and data from other sources pass them to your outside help, names, addresses, and telephone numbers, e-mails of host country referrals you may have, they can sort out who is who or what.

I recommend that you discuss with your outside consultant and share existing market reports, data searched, news and facts about host country and the business conditions in-country. It is also advisable to discuss and draft agreements about the best timing, how, where and who may be involved in the strategy to enter and do business in targeted Latin country.

Remember the less time your consulting help needs to spend on the field, the less the total cost and time will be to your bottom line to start your trade business in Latin America.

Country Risk Evaluation

When I work with new clients in various industries, I spend time, initially networking with Industry Specific networking events and learn about other businesses that may have already venture into Latin America. I always inquiry about their own challenges and successes in particular markets and the benefits or profitability achieved in the chosen country.

The same way, you ought to discover some basic business information affecting entry and what resources need to be allocated in investment and time to have a very good report, opinion and data that the chosen territory will be a good business fit for your product or service. The purpose is to have a very good idea that the potential markets chosen offers and stable business opportunity that is higher than the risk and hazards you have to overcome to be profitable.

Keep in mind that forming joint ventures with local manufacturers or representatives may be beneficial but be clear and get legal counsel on drafting business agreement in English as well as Spanish for most countries and Portuguese for Brazil, spelling out roles in the busines, who retains ownership and control, what percentage of ownership is agreed and is being assigned.

Finding the Best Market for Your Product or Service

You should invest in screening the best market for your company products and service by assessing market demand, potential business, risks and potential revenue. You can do this by doing the following:

1. Obtain Export Statistics. A numbers of publications exist that report the various countries Import-Export indicators that are being currently shipped and are classified by industry and dollar

amounts. You might want to consult the internet as well as Trade associations and Foreign Trade Census numbers that are free resources available to you.

2. Identify the Best Markets. As stated the Latin American region is composed of several countries, you should be able to identify the best 5-10 markets for your product. Check out demand and trends. Realize that some markets may be new to your product or service and may offer little to no competition.

3. Target Markets with Free Trade Agreements. Over the years, the economic impact of trade agreements among nations, has facilitated and ease on import and exports restrictions or increase commerce. Again select a handful of countries that pose the best business opportunity for your business. In U.S. you can consult the internet and a very reliable US Commercial Service, Trade associations, Brokers, Shipping companies and others for references.

4. Product and Services Demand Trends. Look at related goods to yours that can influence demand, calculate demand and forecast. You can consult for local demographic information from Census bureau depending on your industry.

5. Research the Competition. Identify and study market share in your business category in-country which competitors from which countries are players in the market and strategize your business approach to the local market.

6. Other Marketing Factors. Learn how your product can get to market or how the competition is getting it there. Identify channels of distribution, agents, compliance, business practices, pricing policies, size of market demand.

7. Identify Barriers of Entry. Certain countries will tax high their imports than can force you out of market because of high cost of doing business there. Some governments are easy to deal with

because they do not produce those products or services, while others as in the case of Brazil and Argentina, as examples, impose high tariffs to protect local suppliers and control imports.

8. Identify Incentives for Exporting. As is the case of U.S. or some Foreign government that promote international trade, for your product or service, learn about subsidies, tax incentives, export assistance, trade shows, business contacts, official trade and industry missions that are designed to help you enter particular chosen markets because of agreements between countries.

Use available international business trade information tools to do your preliminary research to find out the main markets and industries that are of interest to your business.

Trade Tools and Business Programs

The Trade Americas program offers U.S. based companies the opportunity to look for business opportunities in most Latin American countries combining and exchanging resources and information across the region facilitating trade promotion.

The program is designed to help exporters, this program saves you time, money and resources as it is designed to help you to find Sales and Project opportunities in several countries.

Trade Americas has a website, you can visit: www.buyusa.gov/trade-americas that lists industry specific information, trade events, service providers, business links and other resources and key contacts that will facilitate necessary knowledge so that you can do business, create revenue and profits.

48

Exporting Advice

Recently, in a survey conducted to non-exporter business, it was concluded that they would do international trade if they had information on how to get started in doing business and be able to select and choose best markets, identify buyers and learn about export procedures. As a result, we, in U.S.A. get the benefit that a lot of leg work is already done by our government and essentially, we can determine that they do an excellent job, working for us, with the objective that we do business international.

As you may assume, the governments benefit is to trigger new jobs and strengthen our international trade. The US government is the leading provider of this kind of information for very much all of us to use to our business advantage, visit: www.export.gov or consult with an international trade specialist.

There is a lot of help available at different levels of government for your company through federal, state and local government agencies, trade association and the private sector.

Take a look at the following resources:

The US Commercial Service Export Assistance Center. This agency of the US Department of Commerce maintains a network of international trade specialist in the US ready to help American companies export their products and services.

Export Assistance Centers combine trade, marketing expertise and resources along with financial programs that may include assistance through the Export-Import Bank (Ex-Im Bank) or the Small Business Administration.

These trade specialists work closely with state and local government and private companies that offer international trade expertise, marketing and finance to companies seeking export. They work with their international colleagues to help you get the best and relevant information for your business.

I have used this valuable resource, for years, in working with my own clients, because they can help in:

- Locating and evaluating Latin American buyers, distributors and partners

- Recognize trade and business opportunities

- Provide you with economic statistics, export requirements and compliance documentation

- Export trade finance, foreign market business climate

- International trade shows exhibition, trade missions, export seminars and conferences

- Market research and business counseling

- Research company background checks

- Assisting in making appointments with key people and government officials

- Representations and lobbying on behalf of your American company that may be affected by trade barriers or tenders and help your company become visible to the local market

For further information, visit: www.export.gov

The Export-Import Bank of the United States

The Ex-Im Bank, as is known to business exporters, supports about 80 percent of transactions done by small businesses in the U.S. The Ex-Im Bank offers working capital guarantees and credit insurance for international trade.

These financial services may help your business to increase sales and in entering new markets, offering buyers financing and it may assume up to 90 percent of the lender's risk so exporters can access the necessary funds to purchase or produce U.S. made goods and services for export.

For information on this resource, visit: www.exim.gov

U.S. Trade and Development Agency

The TDA staff develops export marketing programs and obtains industry advice on trade activities. They can help with trade missions, trade fairs, seminars and business counseling. They work directly with companies that manufacture goods and services and help them identify trade opportunities and helps remove obstacles by product or service, industry market and markets.

For further information, visit: www.tda.gov

Bureau of Industry and Security, U.S. Department of Commerce

The bureau of Industry and Security (BIS) is responsible for control of export that deal with national security, foreign policy and specific items with military and commercial applications.

If your product or service falls in this category, you can get assistance for compliance and get permission from BIS Exporter Services in Washington, D.C.

For further information, visit: www.bis.doc.gov

Trade Compliance Center, U.S. Department of Commerce

The Trade Compliance Center (TCC) is part of the U.S. government effort to ensure foreign compliance with trade agreements. This agency monitors, investigates and evaluates compliance with multilateral, bilateral and other overseas trade agreements and standards of business conduct to ensure that U.S. companies received all the benefits of market opening initiatives.

For further information, visit: http://tcc.export.gov

Minority Business Development Agency, U.S. Department of Commerce

The MBDA identifies opportunities for U.S. minority owned business enterprises by promoting their ability to grow and compete in the global economy and selected industries. It also provides information on market and product needs, identifying ways to access education, finance and technology to help minority business succeed.

For further information, visit: www.mbda.gov

Other Export Assistance Resources

- *Small Business Development Centers (SBDC)*, provides a full range of export assistance services to small businesses, especially those in exporting activities.

- *Service Corps of Retired Executives (SCORE)*, provide practical business experience in international trade from most retired corporate executives or previous business owners. They can help you through counseling in very much all matters regarding international trade, they have been there, done that. For information: www.score.org

- *Export Legal Assistance Network (ELAN)*, is a national group of attorneys with international trade experience. For the most part provide initial consultations free to business that are new to exporting or that need export related legal matters. You can visit their site: www.export-legal-assistance.org

- *District Export Councils*, DEC, it's a group of formed by over 1000 businesses and trade experts who volunteer US companies develop solid export strategies by offering workshops and seminars that they sponsor on their own initiative and with help of the Export Assistance Centers.

- *State and Local Governments*, Departments of Commerce, they help with export seminars, Trade Missions that are organized by Mayors or Governors to enable exporters to open new markets and they also participate in Trade Shows under the flag of their City or State in overseas markets and industry events.

- *Financial Institutions*, Banks are very knowledgeable and familiar with specific countries in dealing with various types of products, services and transactions. Large banks located in major U.S. cities maintain business relationships with other banks in foreign countries that may offer direct contacts to foreign customers.

Most international banking specialists are generally well informed about export matters and provide free consultation and guidance to their clients because eventually they will derive revenue and income from export loans, transaction fees, letters of credit and other financial services you may need.

This resource is good because they can guide you with transfer payments, currency exchange, financing exports, issue letters of introduction, credit information on potential buyers and credit assistance to exporter's foreign buyers.

- *Export Agents, Brokers and Intermediaries* offer various services, including market research, appointing and managing distributors and representatives. Additionally, promote and exhibit your products and services at international trade shows, handle shipping and preparing documentation for exports.

  Intermediaries and Agents, like myself, and my company, American Business Links, Corp., work for a number of clients or companies for a sales commission, salary or retainer fee plus commission depending on the product, service or project and the market serviced.

  In using an expert in export matters the company or client gets to market their goods or services right away as experienced professionals can get going faster, in shorter time and be more effective than to have a company develop personnel and resources to handle exports.

- *World Trade Centers, International Trade Clubs, Chambers of Commerce,* are composed by businesspeople that most represent companies engaged in international trade. This may include members like Banks, Shippers, Forwarders, Government Agencies Officials, Custom Brokers, Agents and Distributors.

  These organizations help with educational programs, workshops, networking events and provide critical information regarding market research. Services include, developing trade promotion, overseas missions, mailings, organizing U.S. pavilions for trade shows, providing buyer's contacts, identify distributors and conduct roundtable discussions.

- *American Chambers of Commerce Abroad and Industry Trade Associations* provide valuable market information, handle trade inquiries, recognize actual potential competition, trade needs and business opportunities. (AMCHAM).

  Industry Trade Association can supply detailed information on

54

market demand for products in selected countries, they can refer members to Export Managing Companies (EMC). These associations typically collect and maintain trade news and trends affecting their own industry. For further information, visit: www. uschamber.com

CHAPTER 3

Developing an Export Strategy for Latin America

If you have an ongoing market for your products and services in your own local market, there is also a good chance that consumers in Latin America, if they become aware of them, may pose a new market opportunity and demand for your business. Perhaps, you have a unique product or service that solves the needs of many people or maybe your local market demand is declining and you want to expand and look for new markets. These could be the main reasons why you ought to be looking to open and explore new business in Latin American emerging markets.

Note, however, that companies looking to developing new business, in this region are:

- Export ready companies that have a budget, management team in place or have outside help and are prepared to fund exporting activities over a period of time. Recognize that depending on the product or service and dollar amount of the transaction business can get started and running in a few weeks to months or years depending if there are in-country registrations and other factors.

- Companies and individuals that have a realistic expectation on the return of their investments pursuing new business in Latin America. You cannot look at a market, find out its population and decide you can sell x amount of units, because it does not work like that, because of factors like economic buying power, distribution, spendable income, etc.

- If required companies need to be prepared to modify products and services to adapt to local market requirements and provide after sale support, if they are working directly or train your distributor or agents to provide the local support.

It is helpful to examine your organization vision, direction and decision for export activities, taking in to account the following motivational factors:

- Long term expansion. Building on exporting takes time, money and resources. If you have for quick returns, Latin America is not the place for you to do business, plan for it.

- Competition Advantage. By selling in Latin American or other markets you gain an edge over your competitors understanding and experiencing the complexities and different ways of doing business in the region.

- Increased Capabilities. By stepping in to these territories you might be able to develop new and better products and services by acquiring exposure to the market, dealing with new customers and suppliers and marketing and selling.

- Networking. When in the region you get multiple benefits to customer networks, new technologies, new ideas, develop or introduce other products and services.

- Product Licensing. Some products, technology or services may require special permission, regulations or restrictions. If this is the case you will be at an advantage going into joint ventures for distribution, assembly or manufacturing locally in country.

After Sales Service. Depending on your product or service, ensure that you have trained personnel, agent or local distributor to handle service calls.

Marketing and Distribution Channels to Doing Business in Latin America

There are various ways, you can choose to export your products and market your services, and whichever you do will have a direct impact on your export planning, costs, resources, strategies, time and revenue.

Depending on the level of control, involvement and commitment to the international trade process of your company you can go do the following:

- **Sell to Agents Domestically.** You get the order, wherever your business is located, from an Agent or someone who will pay you directly. You deliver the goods, and in turn, this Agent or Buyer will ship those products to Latin America, as their own. Your company is not involved at all in the export process. For consumer products is straight forward business, if it involves after sales service, technical support or handles end-user or warranty you better trained that Agent or Buyer to deal with their customers.

- **Deal with Brokers.** These are buyers, typically large corporations, middleman, that buy large volume of products from different suppliers in U.S., Asia or Europe, and resell and distribute those products to various retailers chains located in Latin America. They buy from you, they handle the export process and you will see your product on the shelf of a store in another country in a few days or weeks. These, large size and multiple, trade operations have the expertise, know how, and channel of distribution established to get over the hurdles of exporting.

- **Exporting Indirectly through Intermediaries.** Your company hires the services of a firm, like my company American Business Links, Corp. that is capable of finding foreign markets, buyers or distributors for your product or service. Either, Export Management Companies (EMC), Export Trade Companies (ETC), International Trade consultants or Agents, should have the expertise to get you trade contacts, and help you with market entry. EMCs, for the most part, are an effective way for smaller and medium size companies to test the waters of export markets without incurring the costs of full-blown international sales departments. If you are a large organization and do not have an international sales and marketing team in place, EMC's can handle the duties of international trade without interrupting your organization chart, thus offering control, credible and reliable service in handling international trade. These entities and consulting services have been around for a long time and a cost effective export resource.

- **Your Company Exports Directly.** This of course is more challenging because your company has to handle every aspect of the exporting process, including market research, planning, deliveries, registrations, distribution, legal and very important, preparing and presenting proper export documentation and also very important, getting paid!. If your company chooses this path, have the management team in place and committed, allocate resources and investment to run it effectively. While this approach could render more profits and company growth, it will take some time to have it up and running, but many companies involved in international sales have them in-house.

Regardless of the approach you take in reaching Latin American markets, you will need a local presence of some type, either in-country sales representatives, distributors, or a partner, research and choose the best marketing and distribution channel that fits your company objectives.

In-Country Distributors

The role of a distributor, in-country, is to purchase goods or services from your company at a wholesale or discounted price and resell them for profit in their own country. They will handle the importation and the local representation and sales of your products.

In general, these distributors have resources, capital and trained personnel, technical support, warehouse and service the local market. Depending on your product or service these Distributors will offer in-country after sales customer service, technical support, warranty or repairs on your behalf. Usually, they have facilities to stock inventories. Many of these represent other products and services that may or may not compete with your own products or services, depending on the market and market share control.

A substantial number of Distributors, in all industries, attend Industry and Trade Fair shows looking for new products or services to import to their countries. Most of them, in any country, large, medium or small operations exist and usually are part of a business trade association, chambers of commerce or registered at foreign embassies in hopes that when trade missions come to their country they get contacted or invited to participate in trade mission and trade leads.

Attending Trade Shows – Commercial Exhibits Events in America

Trade shows, Fairs or Industry specific events are a very effective, affordable marketing tool that helps you discover the interest of potential buyers, agents and distributors from the Latin America region or other world countries. For years, I have been involved in traveling, attending and exhibiting at American, European and almost all Latin American markets trade shows in various industries and they do work.

When you exhibit you introduce and promote your company products or services. You get the chance to explore who else is a player or competitor in your industry and you get an appreciation for business potential.

If you are ready for exhibition, do it right away, ensuring domestic and international visibility, send out invitations, web promotion and emails to prospects. Depending on your industry, there are a few events year round in various countries and usually a Main Event for your own industry that happens once a year that gathers domestic and international visitors. Consult with your Industry Association of your Product or Service and capitalize on exhibiting, if you cannot exhibit, then do attend these events and network.

When you decide to exhibit start by gathering pertinent information for the show: Dates of the event, location, costs for exhibition, size of exhibit space booth, previous and projected, demographics, and business contacts from which country has come, arranging travel and hotels reservations, plan to attend networking events, learn about the do's and do not's of exhibiting and restrictions, compliance or especial requirements for showcasing your product or service, logistics, literature, displays, booth design and rules and regulations prospectus.

Attending these exhibits, require planning, budget allocation and having personnel to help your business exposure and promotion during the event to gather leads. While some events will allow you to sell directly from your booth, other events may be more restrictive as to what you can and cannot do during the trade event. Remember that all depends on the location, country and culture, keep in mind these trade events are a Business Lead Generation tool event.

While traveling to attend these events, for various industries in U.S. cities, European and Latin American events, I have witnessed how the different cultures impact the nature of the exhibit. For instance, in U.S. trade shows, it is more restrictive per say to having or serving alcohol on the exhibit booth premises, you may need to have a liquor license or outsource that service to entertain your visitors. And trade shows in Europe passing beer, wine or champagne is accepted and expected. But in some Latin American countries, you may have hostesses or models passing beer, wine, champagne and liquor as means of getting visitors to stop by a booth. The objective of course is to get the attention and exposure of business people to stop by, gather their information that eventually will lead to business dealings.

The point is I want to make is, if you are going to exhibit at industry specific trade shows or fairs, do it right. Seek the experience and tips of the exhibit organizing committee. In no way I suggest that having gimmicks like hiring gorgeous models should overpower the value of your product or service or you must invest in filling the thirst for an alcoholic beverage of the attendees, but depending on the event and culture that may be suggested to attract new customers.

CHAPTER 4

Business Structure in Pursuing Business in Latin America

If you are planning to export directly and sell to end users, government, agents or deal with in-country distributors, you might want to set an office, initiate a joint venture or set up a local subsidiary operation, you will be required to form and register your business in the host-country that meets the legal requirements of the country.

In U.S.A., as an example, you set up a business and your run with it right away without much bureaucracy, you do not especial licenses to import or export, unless you are dealing with certain products and services regulated by our government, however, be aware that many countries require that you obtain an import or export licenses that can only be granted to locally registered business. This is sometimes, as it is an already long bureaucracy you have to overcome. Try to get the advice of legal consul for these matters to be in compliance.

Due to local customs and regulations, many countries forbid foreigners from holding controlling interest in domestic companies, even if it is your own company. Many will allow foreign companies or individuals to form and enter into legal business, as long as a local national, individual citizen or company joins in with you. Of course, a way around this is to get someone to sign in with you, then, once the company is set up, have them turn their interest holdings back to you for the majority shares or 100 percent control of the company and its operations.

Export Managing Companies (EMC) or in-country trade agents can help you charter these waters of local bureaucracy and recommend the best business structure for your business consulting with local experience attorneys and consultants so that you can operate freely and in compliance with local laws and regulations and look for Tax incentives to set up your business in-country, seek joint-venture partnerships or even possibly alienate your business with the government, as a partner, when your product, project or service calls for it.

Here are series of questions about business structure and ownership concerns that need to be answered:

- What are the in-country laws that relate to foreign business ownership

- What is the best business form, a Corporation, Partnership or Joint Venture

- What are the restrictions or benefits on each form of business

- Do local laws require a host-country individual or corporation partner in a joint venture or other strategic alliance

- If a local partner is required, what percentage of ownership must you give up to set up the business and what roles will be played out regarding who handles business liabilities, control and operation

- Trade names, formulas, know how, registration and copyrights how is handled in-country and who retains ownership

Distributor, Agent or Representative Checklist

After reviewing the various options and channels of distribution for your product or service, what in essence you need to look for are that the people or business you are dealing with have the following:

66

- Experience with your industry, product or service in-country

- A sales and marketing organization

- An established business with clients or new prospects

- Knowledge of marketing, business contacts or business relationships in country

- After sales service capability

- Internet web presence

- Financial references and payment history

- Able to communicate in English via phone or writing emails or faxes

Tax, Legal, Audit and Licensing

If you are looking to set up an in-country operation, checking with your legal and accounting counsel ought to direct you to get critical and invaluable information that pertains to legal, taxes, accounting and licensing information. This searched information may include the reference to someone's name, telephone number or resident business partners which can educate you right away on local laws and steps in getting legal and accounting compliance.

Licensing, given rights, for in-country partners to develop, manufacture, assemble or distribute your product or service could an alternative, as well, but you ought to consult with your own legal counsel as well as the in-country legal team how to draft and what to include in the agreement and not get lost in the translation. This requires more due diligence on your part to prevent copying, or share profits and royalties back to you.

The advisors you hire should inform you on the following matters:

- Tax Information Exchange Agreement between host country and your own country

- Tax rates, incentives or exemptions for corporations doing business in-country

- Are there any restrictions or taxes to repatriate earnings or royalties, take back your profits

- Import taxes and tariffs and retail tax collecting and filing reports

- Legal reports and income and revenue declarations to appointed government agencies

Let's be clear, that I am not a Tax or Legal counselor but over the past few years, new economic reforms in various countries, have created very at times more legal hurdles and bureaucratic systems in all Latin American countries. There are laws governing contracts, taxes and the protection of intellectual property rights when you have a very unique product or service that you have to be aware of how to handle to engage in the proper trade agreement and with whom.

Business permits, licenses and product registrations and other related international business topics continue changing. The compliance of one country's law may be very different from the country next border. Be aware, that many court systems for business matters, litigations or arbitration are not as modern or easy to deal with, as is the case of European or American legal processes. For instance, I you planning to sue for breach of contract, payment or violation of product or service intellectual rights, do not attempt to do it remotely or do it alone, it will serve you to hire experts on the field to represent your company's interest.

Latin American Government Subsidies

Direct subsides of incentives and programs are available from many Latin American countries to attract foreign investment and trade. It makes sense for their own local economy to create jobs and opportunities. Depending on the type of business you are involved in, you might want to learn the subsidies that the countries are offering, that they may have available and may be of interest to your business.

Some subsidies may consist of the following:

- Exemption from income and other taxes

- Some may offer, low-interest, long-term financing

- Special funding to train your own labor

- Exemption from import customs duties to bring your technology to set up the business

- May have rent-free housing for foreign executives

- May be able to take All your profits tax free out of the country

You can find out from Embassies and Consulates in your own country information about these incentives. In-country Ministry of Finance and related Government Agency can offer you information as well. As in the case of U.S. some of those programs can be researched easily as they may be part of an economic reform plan to work with a particular country, region or industry.

Not everyone business that wants to set up shop in a particular country is automatically entitled to get those incentives, in most cases, while those incentives may be available, they are negotiated on a case by case basis. It is better to let your local attorney, agent or legal representative to negotiate and draft those agreements.

In country, U.S. Embassies, trade personnel can point you in the right direction by offering you reports on the current status of government to government relationships, investment opportunities, subsidies and incentives, thus creating trade flow to both countries.

Latin America Market-Specific Business Conditions

In many businesses through much of Latin American and Caribbean countries or cities, and in certain specific industries, there are groups, individuals, families or cartels that control the majority of the business. Some of these groups, companies, individuals or cartels may be linked through a tight web of cross-holdings companies or informal and enforceable businesses agreements that will ease or difficult entry.

Depending on the product, service or project you are bringing to their Latin American country, these groups operate with the closed eye of their government and can influence and impose business restrictions or limitations. Too often, this invisible groups exercise the success, delay, or no-entry, of your product or service, in their market.

Business cartels and controlled industries have a direct impact on market conditions, demands and pricing. When competing with local produced goods or similar quality it is very difficult that an imported product will compete on price. Cartels, labor unions or industry associations have been known to block the sale of imported goods that may have higher technology, better quality, or modern styles, just because 'they can' and have the resources, and political cloud and power to do it.

Each country has a handful of these influential interests groups, recognizing this from the get go will help you which direction to take in exploring business in their country, ignoring this fact may be devastating to your business, so be aware and look for profitable business opportunities and agreements.

If it looks as this type of group pressure exist to get your business blocked in entering their country, better look to seek new business somewhere else. Top officials in government or private industries will not admit publicly to such informal barriers, however, they do exist. This is not a founded critic on Latin America culture, it happens in many cities and countries around the world.

The same is true, in America, where the good, 'old boy network' exists in certain industries, like oil, pharmaceutical and Defense Industries, however, these networks are not as evident as in certain parts of South and Central America and the entire Caribbean, stretching across wide range of industries and businesses.

Recognize that personal relationships among sales representatives, bankers, bureaucrats, lawyers, and accountants create a steady cross current of preferential treatment and favors, every one that has visited these region has experience this from standing in line at the airport arrival, government office or banks. Who knows who and things get done right away.

Your objective early in the trade effort is to identify such power individual, companies or government officials to set the appropriate groundwork and you can have smooth way through customs, establishing bank relations, government compliance and the green light to do business.

If you venture in learning if this people or groups exist, just ask some government official, bankers, lawyers, consultants or accountants and they will point you in the right direction, as they exchange contacts and businesses and are up to speed on dealings and transactions taking place.

Assessing the Competition

Your market research should be extensive to learn the names of competitors, along with their estimated market share control and potential business revenue that they generate from in-country sales.

A good place to start is the local Chamber of Commerce or the in-country American Chamber of Commerce, for the most part, they have access to members and company profiles and who their executives are. This information helps their own member to know about pricing, presence and commercial activities.

If your competition comes from other American or European sources and such competition is firmly entrenched, it may pay you to join forces with one of these companies in some form of alliance, a joint venture, licensing, distribution or some other business structure agreement that will make your business thrive. Two importers working together may be able to capture a large market share than either could so separately, especially when competing with local suppliers and the constant threat of cheap, low quality Asian products.

Transport of Goods and Security

If you are looking to be in charge of handling cargo to its final in-county destination, or perhaps you are planning to set up an assembly or manufacturing company, a great place to start securing information for local transportation is a local trading company.

When you inquiry with these companies ask about transportation availability, roads, tariffs, security concerns, especially when equipment, raw materials availability or transport finished product overland. Rates and tariffs, trucking lines, and on-loading and off-loading requirements from one contract hauler to another, varies.

When transporting goods in-country learn about alternatives for inland shipping, inland transport permits, import licenses, recommended security measures, sources of raw materials, and the availability and cost of labor and management personnel involved in ensuring an in-country local production or run a distribution facility. Be aware, where, when, how much are raw materials, supplies, and production equipment requirements for your operation, are they available locally, or will they have to be imported from the United State or other countries? If import licenses or permits required, and how do you get them?

It is not uncommon that either you or your local transport company will be involved in payoffs when transporting your goods, to and from in-country to your facility or at the ports of entry. Customs personnel will tell you about on loading and off loading procedures as well as duties to be paid. Whenever possible outsource the transportation of your cargo, this way the responsibility, liability, security assistance rest on your service provider while you get proper insurance. Better to be protected than sorry.

Dealing with Corruption, Bribery and Political Government Changes

Lets define first what Corruption and Bribery means, is an action to secretly provide a good or a service to a third party so that he or she can influence certain actions which benefit the corrupt, a third party, or both in which the corrupt agent has authority. A moral deviation from an ideal, this may include activities like bribery or embezzlement. Usually, when an office-holder, or government employee, acts in an official capacity for personal gain.

Petty cooperation occurs at a smaller scale and within established social frameworks and governing norms. Examples include the exchange of small improper gifts or use of personal connections to obtain favors. This form of corruption is particularly common in developing countries and where public servants are significantly underpaid.

Grand corruption is defined as corruption occurring at the highest levels of government in a way that requires significant subversion of the political, legal and economic systems. Such corruption is commonly found in countries with authoritarian or dictatorial governments but also in those without adequate policing of corruption.

The government system in many countries is divided into the legislative, executive and judiciary branches in an attempt to provide independent services that are less prone to corruption due to their independence, however, there are government loops or government agencies that work much like independent business operations.

Systemic corruption is corruption which is primarily due to the weaknesses of an organization or process. It can be contrasted with individual officials or agents who act corruptly within the system.

Bribery is the improper use of gifts and favors in exchange for personal gain. This is also known as kickbacks and is the most common form of corruption. The types of favors given are diverse and include money, gifts, sexual favors, company shares, entertainment, employment and political benefits. The personal gain that is given can be anything from actively giving preferential treatment to having an indiscretion or crime overlooked. Bribery can sometimes be part of a the systemic use of corruption for other ends, for example to perpetrate further corruption. Bribery can make officials more susceptible to blackmail or extortion.

Corruption, not matter how you describe it, the fact, it exist and is alive, the common 'greasing of the hands', the 'pact's behind close doors', the promises of gains for votes, favor, or gain approval for a particular project, understand that it happens when dealing, primarily with government entities, not matter where you are in Latin America.

Over the years the amounts of corruption and political instability in the region had prevented many foreign companies to doing business in Latin America. Some countries have improved ways to have more transparency in their government dealings, while other countries, depending on the project, dollar amount and who sits in office or political power in charge will manage and agree on things in closed doors meeting, away from public scrutiny and the media.

Stories of bribes and kickbacks paid to bureaucrats, military, customs personnel, and law enforcement officials has happen and in certain countries is the norm. However, I am making you alert that these things tend to happen but you should not take part in it. Specifically when large infrastructure projects are proposed or high technology projects are brought to government owned control, government financed, or government approved, bureaucratic corruption must be calculated in to the bid prices.

This environment of corruption is of course in the government dealings for the most part. If your company is selling energy solutions, infrastructure projects, bridges, power, water plants, and the like, leave it to the locals to sort out how things will be handle and paid. Do not get involved, other than to work and be on the 'winning side'.

In many cases, if you look to get on national or international tenders, even getting to play or be on the bidder's list will cost money. Focus mainly that if your local folks win the project, they pay you for your goods and services and leave the rest to them. Best if you are not directly in those agreements or your company as this can compromise you and there are laws in place against corruptive practices. If you are required to par take on these meetings, get the advice from your counsel before making any verbal or written offers for payment, commissions or referrals.

Political Changes happen every 4, 5 or 6 years typically in most countries when new elections take place. Be alert and concerned about the timing in working, and who you should be working with before submitting a bid for a project. Once you submit a bid, what looked like a stable environment when you started could easily turn out to be just the opposite, because of what political party s in charge, by the time you actually begin working on the project. This means you would have to start all the process again dealing with the people who are or will be in charge of running the city, region or country.

My advice and suggestion is to let the locals folks with their strategic alliances do the work, stay out of politics, refrain from agreements that you will not be able to handle and deliver what you have been contracted to do, when they win the bid. If you stay out of politics and focus on your b business, then you will be dealing and perhaps profit more from areas where, you personally, do not want to be in.

Many contracting companies, American, European or Asian, are participants of large infrastructure projects in Latin America, so instead of your seeking direct deals with local governments, contact them, if your product or service fits their profile or, bidding requirements or proposals, they can carry all the risk, pay bribes, hire subcontractors, deal with the government so that you can stay out and minimize your exposure and get your profit share of the project to the extent of the value of your product or service.

By working as a subcontractor, you are shielded by the prime contractor from the vagaries of corruption and political upheaval. This provides an excellent opportunity for smaller and mid-size companies to reap the benefits of infrastructure projects with little risk, and just supply the equipment, parts, service, products, management and technical know-how, or labor to build the project, and that is it.

If you or your company is from U.S. be aware of a new law, the Sarbanes-Oxley Act of 2002, which was enacted to attack off-the-books bribes or kickbacks given to foreign government officials, and is enforced by the U.S. Department of Justice. All U.S. companies, large or small, must be aware of these laws and have policies on the books to be certain that employees abide by them. In dealing with many Latin America countries and government, despite of what U.S. laws say regarding corruption practices, bribes are a way of life. But, be aware of legal consequences for you and your business and how it can affect you.

CHAPTER 5

The Good, the Bad and the Ugly of Latin America

Now that we had covered an overview of the region and business opportunities to have in Latin-American, I would like to recap the following points that are foremost in many people's minds when it comes to dealing with this region:

What are the benefits of working in Latin America?

Everywhere you go in Latin-America you will encounter a rich and colorful history. From their early beginnings and the settlement of the people indigenous to the land, the influences of the European explorer's and trader's, through the growth and change that has influenced the people's lives there is much to see and experience.

For the most part you will encounter people who are genuinely warm and welcoming. In many countries you will find yourself visiting the home of a client. Then of course you have the wonderful food, delightful music, and, in many cases, a vibrant and relaxed lifestyle. On the business side in most Latino countries respect and honesty are important values and your word is as strong as whatever you write on paper.

While you will find that most of the people you do business with speak English, however, it would not hurt your ability to achieve success if you were even a small bit conversant in the Spanish or Portuguese language of your host country.

Is Working in those Countries Safe?

On the downside a factor to be considered when discussing the safety of a given country include its crime rate. Certainly anyone traveling to a foreign country needs to be both aware of the potential for crime and what they can do to protect themselves.

The crime rate in Latin-America is double the world average. It is estimated by the Inter-American Development Bank that the high crime rate in many Latin-American countries has a significant impact on their Gross Domestic Product (GDP). In human costs, murder, crimes against women, drug and gang related crimes are the most common forms of crime.

While anyone spending time in a Latino country needs to be aware of where they are it should be noted that your chance of being a victim of a criminal act in Latin-America is no higher than in cities like St. Louis, Detroit, and Chicago. Here are some tips to make your travel safer when you go and visit Latin American countries:

- Do not travel to unknown or unfamiliar parts of any city you are in

- Whenever possible be in the company or care of your host to go out, picked up or drop off to your hotel

- Do not wear clothing, jewelry, or drive an auto that makes it seem as though you are a rich American or Foreigner

- Remain aware of your surroundings

- Do not take it upon yourself to go further within the country than you feel safe doing

78

- As anywhere else, if you sense danger or feel threatened; leave that area immediately

- If you feel safer, upon arrival at your destination notify the American Embassy of your whereabouts

- Check with the U.S. Department of State for information about your safety before leaving for your destination

Does it Make any Sense to Do business in Latin-America?

At first glance probably not. But it is important to look beneath the surface of crime and corruption. The real Latino countries consist of thriving economies, millions of consumers wanting American and Foreign goods, an amazing wealth of natural resources, and many governments working hard at changing the high crime rates of their country. These pluses should not be overlooked.

Get to know as much as you can about the country you will be in.

Pricing and Terms of

You must consider having an export product pricing strategy that will differ from your domestic sales. Most Latin American countries are price sensitive markets, therefore, it can be the most challenging to establish since there are so many variables to consider, shipping costs, time, import tariffs and taxes, competition, etc. and then, establishing a Terms of Sale to get paid.

In calculating pricing start by calculating the manufacturing cost, administration and overhead, research and development, freight forwarding, custom charges, distributor margins and your profit and stay in range to be competitive in the market.

Other costs that you will add to the mix, depending on the product and service are the expenses for your business to conduct credit and market research, travel expenses, translation, commissions and legal or expert advice to get your business established in Latin America.

Regarding Terms of Sale and negotiation with your potential distributor or client are the way in you quote pricing. In the international market, pro forma quotations are issued utilizing Incoterms 2000 (International Commercial Terms).

For further information about this reference, consult: www.iccbooksusa.com. This book list the terms and their definition, for instance the most common terms used are:

- CIF, means cost, insurance and freight to destination port. Usually used for shipments by ocean. Your client for the declared value on the pro forma invoice will get the goods at the port and from there client will pay import tariffs and taxes.

- FOB, means free on board, refers to the price quoted in the country of origin of the shipment. It includes the costs for loading the goods on board a vessel.

- EXW, ex-works, this means that your are quoting the price only at the point of origin, the seller's premises, factory or warehouse).

Additionally to these above terms, you have CFR, CPT, FAS, FCA and others consult the Incoterms guidelines, but whenever you see an "F" term is the seller's responsibility to clear the goods for export from the country of origin.

It is important to understand and use sales terms correctly to avoid misunderstandings and shipping costs obligations calculations and logistics. Whenever, possible quote in U.S. dollars to avoid the risk of exchange rate fluctuations and currency conversion.

Consult with your Freight Forwarder for assistance in figuring out Incoterms when quoting to your buyers. Provide to them with information of the product exported, weight, size so your Freight Forwarder can help you compute pricing accordingly.

Shipping Your Product

When shipping your goods to Latin America, be aware of packing, labeling, documentation, insurance and regulation compliance.

My advice is to establish a very good business communication and relationship with an experienced International Freight Forwarder that can help you in moving your products to country of destination. They are savvy in export regulations, shipping options, import rules and regulations of foreign countries and documentation required in Foreign Trade.

A reliable Freight Forwarder should be licensed by the International Air Transport Association (IATA) to handle air freight and the Federal Maritime Commission to handle ocean freight.

- **In Packing for Export:** Be aware of shipping and packing your products that guarantees your goods will arrive in one piece, by safeguarding packaging that prevents breakage, leakage, movement, moisture, pilferage and excess weight.

- **Labeling:** These exported goods must be Labeled and Marked for export in cartoon, pallets or containers that meets export shipping regulations. These labels will include: country of origin, weight, special marks and symbols, caution and handling instructions, etc.

- **Documentation:** I will recommend that your Freight Forwarder handle the export documentation, they know this process very well and can help you avoid mistakes, delays, penalties or even loss of shipments.

Freight Forwarders can help you in preparing and handling proper documentation, and are critical in compliance and meeting export/ import requirements, for instance:

- When shipping by Air Freight they can issue air waybills.

- Bill of Lading, is a contract between the owner of the goods and the carrier.

- Commercial Invoice, is a bill for the goods from the seller to the buyer.

- Certificate of Origin, when required by some countries this document must show that the goods come from the place you said it is from and usually validated by Government Agency or Chamber of Commerce.

- NAFTA certificate of origin is required for products traded between the countries where the importer is claiming zero-duty preference.

- An Export Packing List, that details the information about the goods shipped and itemized amounts, weight and size dimensions.

- Insurance Certificate is to assure that the consignee that insurance will cover the loss or damage to the cargo during transit.

- An Export License is a government issued document that authorizes the export of specific controlled goods and quantities to a particular destination or government.

When it comes to shipping handling, transportation and freight insurance rely on the expertise of your own Freight Forwarder to have a successful export and transfer of cargo to the buyer's destination country.

Methods of Payment

When dealing with Latin American countries your business should extend credit, when appropriate. Always, evaluate and qualify the credit worthiness and risk of your buyer.

Everyone knows, Cash is King, everywhere. However, depending on the size of the transaction, volume, frequency of orders and dollar amounts will dictate the best payment method, including Cash in Advance, Letter of Credit, Open Account, Document collection or draft, Consignment.

- **Cash in Advance:** Receiving cash by means of a direct bank deposit, check or wire transfer is ideal. There is not collection of payment problems, you get the money first then you ship the goods and repeat the sales cycle.

- **Letters of Credit:** This documents issued by financial institutions after qualifying the buyer credit worthiness of the value of the transaction, protects the buyer and the seller. The letter list the steps and responsibility of each and when both sides are in compliance with the terms of Letter of Credit, bank ensure the buyer that the seller has complied and that the buyer is satisfied with shipment and Letter is cashed and paid to seller by the financial institution from corresponding bank. The Letter of credit adds the bank's promise to the buyer to pay the exporter. Some Letters of Credit add the term, Irrevocable, which means it cannot be changed unless both parties agree, and Revocable Letter of Credit which may carry many risks to the exporter as either party may unilaterally make changes to their favor.

Always seek your Banker look over these documents to ensure validity of payment upon exporting.

- **Open Account:** This can be a convenient method of payment when you have an established buyer business relationship or you have checked their creditworthiness or the terms of negotiation according to the nature of the goods and services you export.

- **Consignment Sales:** This method means simply that you ship the goods and when your foreign distributor sells them, they pay you. You the exporter carry all the risk and may take a while to get paid, it is the least favored way of doing business in Latin America.

Eliminate, reduce or avoid payment problems when dealing with exports of your goods. I advice that you conduct credit checks, establish trusted and responsible business relationships to ensuring getting paid.

Because in the event buyer's default or delay for whatever reason, collecting payment can be very difficult, time consuming and more expensive than the amount of the transaction defaulted. I can add, on this topic, that Selling is not problem, everyone will buy from you, the challenge many times is getting paid. I also advice when available get payment Credit Insurance to protect your export. As usual, exercise business prudence in exporting and when extending payment terms, know how you will get paid.

Extended Credit Terms

Latin America credit reports tend to be outdated, inaccurate and unregulated or non-existent in some countries. The U.S. Commercial Service can be very helpful, as one it's missions, is to help small and mid-size U.S. exporters. They can provide you with an opinion as to the viability and reliability of the overseas company or individual you have selected as well as an opinion on the relative strength of that company's industry sector in your target market.

The U.S. Commercial Service can help you obtain this report by issuing an International Company Profile (ICP) background. These reports include:

- A credit standing report on prospective Latin American target customers, prospective partners and distributors

- Reference and verification of the company's officers and senior management

- Banking and other financial information about the company

- Market information, sales, market share, and even profit history and market presence

Commercial banks offer a credit information on virtually any customer who has purchased goods from an American company with the past few years to determine credit and payment history.

Trade Finance

If your company can offer trade finance, assuming you have done your search and have a good business partner, this can be critical, to a profitable exporting activity. Nine times out of ten, the amount of financing you offer determines whether you or your competitor gets the business.

As a marketing tool, trade finance provides a competitive advantage, the same as other advantages like offering price discounts, after-the-sale customer service or free deliveries.

Depending on the customer and country, customized trade finance strategies may be necessary. Again, beware of defaulting risk, and since collections can be difficult, get credit insurance. You can get credit insurance to cover losses from customers who refuse to pay, political expropriation, breach of contract, and other causes.

It is possible to do business in Latin America without credit insurance, YES, but if credit insurance is available, get it, and add to the cost of doing business, reduce your risk.

Selling with E-commerce in Latin America

This form of business is defined as, any commercial transaction facilitated by the exchange of information electronically. Everyone now days use the internet for research, communication, business, education or other uses including the purchases of goods or services over the internet.

The World Wide Web has open frontiers, and reaches many corners of the globe directly to consumers. Online business has grown a lot in Latin America over the past few years, between merchants and consumers, while there is retails sales the chance for wholesale also do exist.

While it is true that business online can be profitable and run from your business office or your bedroom, be aware that retails sales from Latin America can be limited due to antiquated banking systems and lack of use of credit cards, some connectivity internet problems and of course the challenge of shipping your goods to end consumer to their in-country address.

Many businesses use the internet to promote their goods and services to get the attention of the market and use that data to seek the best suitable business partner to sell their goods and services in-country. This is an effective marketing tool to acquire customers because is cheaper to set up and promote. Many customers become aware of your merchandise and pricing and compare it to local prices.

There are many advantages to using the Internet for your business, for example, the ability to bypass middleman, agents, distributors or in-country retail chains, but depending on the product or service you provide, ensure that your product or service is in compliance with local laws to ship it and get cleared by customs to be delivered to your customer.

How to Import and Sell in the United States of America

Importing is the opposite of Exporting, it means that we bring merchandise, from a foreign country for use, sale, processing, re-export, or to acquire and use services in to U.S. territory.

Just about any international company wants to target and looks forward to doing business with the largest and richest market in the world, the United States of America, a 300 Million economic super power spread over 50 states. Recognize that this is a very large market and some areas or cities in the U.S. are as large as one or many countries economies combined.

May I suggest that you review or look at the strategies exposed covered at the beginning of this book, on How to Export section and implement some of those strategies to your commercial efforts to Import in to U.S.

Once you identify that you have a demand for your product or want to establish a demand for your product, select and work with the distribution channel that will make your product or service accessible to the market.

If you are an American citizen or U.S. resident most likely you will need to set up a legal entity in your own state and seek the assistance of a Freight Forwarding company or Customs Broker to help you set up your Import trade activity.

If you are a Foreigner looking to capitalize on the U.S. market, please read the Export section of this book and apply strategies to bring your products or services to U.S. There are plenty of programs in Latin America to help you seek U.S. markets for your products or services, but is equally important to determine if you will be setting up your own office in U.S., seek the advice of a U.S. attorney and accountant to be in compliance, or seek partnership, or distributorships with companies that have an established network of distribution channels, buyers or retailers.

Programs like NAFTA (North American Free Trade Agreement), CAFTA-DR (Central American Free Trade Agreement and Dominican Republic) and other government international commerce agreements between nations are facilitating the export and import transactions with U.S. market thus creating more business opportunities for your product or service to find its way in U.S. soil.

There are of course other Latin American commerce agreements you ought to consult, if your contry falls within, Association of Caribbean States, Caribbean Commom Market (CariCom), CariCom Bolivia, CariCom Venezuela, Mercosur (Souther Cone Common Market), Central American Commom Market and others.

These trade agreements will help you create advantages and ease the process of compliance with U.S. regulations and incentives. Start locally seeking your own government initiative Export Initiatives, Chambers of Commerce or Industry Associations, Consultants.

I highly encourage you also that you start with your own in-country or foreign based shipping Forwarder company, they can offer you real experience advice. Independent Agents, Consultants also will be of great benefit to you in navigating existing regulations imposed by various U.S. government agencies that deal with international trade.

For instance, depending on the goods or services you want to sell in U.S. territory you will be exchanging information and complying with U.S. Customs, Free trade zones, custom bonded warehouses, brokers,

Homeland Security, World Customs Organization, Immigration, Border Patrol and Surety Bonds.

Importing and Negotiations with American Businesses

As we have seen in this writing, dealing with Latin Americans is based mostly on relationships, the touch and feel good, before business, while in dealing with Americans, in general, business comes first. While bargaining and establishing price agreements is most common in Latin America, the U.S. usually operates on a fixed price system. Buyers, regardless of their socio economic status, are used to accept the products and services as offered and pay the price asked for it.

Most Latinos regard Americans are being 'cold' or 'too cold', the reality is culturally, educationally we might be different and in many large metropolitan cities, the touch and feel good of relationships, are normally found in pocket areas of U.S. in the South, Mid West or rural areas. Cities like New York, Los Angeles, Chicago, as examples, 'time is money', life move at a faster pace and we might not show the same courtesies that you are used to back in your own country. You came to U.S. for business, come and get the business, things are not taken personal, is just business.

In negotiating with Americans, show how much quantity, units need to be sold and how that number will reflect on the revenue sheet and how much is left on the bottom line to their business, and how the customer benefits and give assurances of after sales customer service. If you do not have the means of handling your own Imports in U.S., my advice is to get a competent distributor, agent or wholesaler to handle the distribution of your products or services. You focus on manufacture and delivery, and leave the marketing and sales to the Americans, whether these 'Americans' are American or of Latin American descent,

91

as long as they are living and doing business in U.S. and complying with local customs and laws affecting the business.

Additionally, probably back in your own Latin country your product or service is already in demand, there is a likelihood that your product may be in demand also here in the Community of fellow citizens that live in U.S., find out where they are and sell to them. For instance, if I was selling a product or service from Colombia I would look for the Colombian markets in NY, Miami and upcoming Orlando where many of them reside. If from El Salvador, then go to Washington, D.C., or if from Mexico, Chicago, Los Angeles and Houston would be great places to look at.

Almost ALL countries from Latin America are represented in large numbers in different states and cities. That makes your business search easier. Seek other business products or services marketed in those areas and seek those channels of distribution to get to your own market.

If you are after the 'American market' then will recommend you do due diligence, research, invest and identify or create the demand for your product and go for it. Americans love business as much as you do.

Keep in mind, as you might already know, the United States of America is full of laws and attorneys. The costs of doing business here are higher and liability on the product or service is always a major concern to the supplier because the consumer in U.S. is well protected, by established policies of return, guarantees, warranties, after sell service and overall customer satisfaction.

Some of the things that Americans will expect from you in seeking to Import thru partnerships or distributorships are: Exclusivity, protected territories, credit terms or discounts, freedom to price, the right to terminate agreement, good warranties, product availability, manufacturing and supplying capabilities. Ensure you can meet the demand of the market.

The World Customs Organization

This organization, known as WCO has been in existence for more than 50 years and have established guidelines to Harmonized the world's customs procedures to increase prosperity among nations and international trade. WCO at major international convention created and administer guidelines, like the following:

- Harmonized System Convention (A guideline for U.S. import and export schedules that feature a number that identifies the industry and product with a particular serial number in a table that exempts or charges taxes on imports)

- 1973 Kyoto Convention on customs procedures

- 1999 Revised Kyoto Convention, International Convention on Harmonization and Simplification of Customs Procedures

- GATT Customs Valuation Agreement

The WCO alongside U.S. Customs and Border Protection (CBP) agencies have drafted guidelines and standards relating to the security of international supply chains.

For further information on how these guidelines affect or classified your product in to U.S. market consult and visit: www.cbp.gov and look up, the Harmonized Commodity Description and Coding System, also known as the Harmonized System (HS), of tariff nomenclature is an internationally standardized system of names and numbers for classifying traded products.

INCOTERMS 2010

The Incoterms rules or International Commercial Terms are a series of pre-defined commercial terms published by the International Chamber of Commerce that are widely used in International commercial transactions or procurement processes. A series of three-letter trade terms related to common contractual sales practices, the Incoterms rules are intended primarily to clearly communicate the tasks, costs, and risks associated with the transportation and delivery of goods.

The Incoterms rules are accepted by governments, legal authorities, and practitioners worldwide for the interpretation of most commonly used terms in international trade. They are intended to reduce or remove altogether uncertainties arising from different interpretation of the rules in different countries. As such they are regularly incorporated into sales contracts worldwide.

When you agree to sell, quote or ship one of the following Standard Trade Definitions used in INCOTERMS for any mode or modes of transportation will be mentioned. Here we mention only a few, as examples and its meanings:

FOB – Free on Board. Once the goods have passed over the ship's rail at the port of export the Buyer is responsible for all costs and risks of loss or damage to the goods from that point.

EXW – Ex Works. The buyer pays all transportation costs and also bears the risks for bringing the goods to their final destination.

CFR – Cost and Freight. The seller must pay the cost and freight required in bringing the goods to the named port of destination.

CIF – Cost, Insurance and Freight. The seller has the same obligations as under CFR, however, it requires to provide insurance against the buyer's risk of loss or damage to the goods during transit.

Other common terms: FCA, Free Carrier. CPT, Carriage Paid To. DDP, Delivered Duty Paid. FAS, Free Alongside Ship. CIP, Carriage and Insurance Paid.

Homeland Security

The department organization came in to existence in 2002 to mobilize and organize the U.S. to secure itself from terrorist attacks.

You can find the department's mission, goals, operation and prevention activities by visiting www.dhs.gov and see how you product or service is in compliance to be imported to U.S.

Immigration and Customs Enforcement (ICE)

This entity created in 2003 became the largest investigative branch of the Department of Homeland Security (DHS). It combines the law enforcement of the Immigration and Naturalization Service (INS) and the former U.S. Customs Service to protect the country from terrorist attacks. You can learn more visiting, www.ice.gov

Within the scope of their activities are to: To check people, money, materials that may support criminal or terrorist acts, dismantling gang organizations, seizing financial assets, fraudulent immigration applications, investigates illegal exports of controlled technology, helps combat the smuggle and traffic of humans in to U.S. territory, targets criminal organizations responsible for producing, smuggling and distributing counterfeit products.

Customs and Border Protection Service (CBP)

It was created in 1789 and is responsible for enforcement of trade. The major responsibility is the administration of the Tariff Act of 1930 that includes:

- Enforcing laws against smuggling

- Collecting all duties, taxes and fees for the entry of cargo in more than 300 U.S. ports

- Release, classification and valuation of imported merchandise

- Impose fines, penalties and forfeitures

- Processing and entry of passengers into the U.S. territory

- Other activities related to trade and international travel

To obtain information about its functions and operations, visit: www.cbp.gov or www.customs.gov. This entities are responsible for trade compliance (import) passenger operations, outbound operations (exports) and implement anti-smuggling strategies.

Customs Brokers

Whenever you need to import in to U.S. you will need the services of one. Just as the Freight Forwarder is a good source of information and will help you with documentation and compliance, the Custom Broker is a private service company licensed to assist importers in the movement of their goods to U.S.

This private service is a liaison between the Customs Service Agency and the Importing Companies. Entries of foreign goods and duty collections are managed by Custom Brokers on behalf of importers. All of them are licensed and regulated by the U.S. Treasure Department.

Importers hire the services of a Custom Broker as their Agent who usually handles all documentation, answer questions, collect import duties and deals, directly, with the Custom Service.

I recommend that, if you do not have a Custom Broker, consult and locate through references or yellow pages, an experience and established Custom Broker that can support you and handle all technical questions regarding your imports, from filing entry documents, getting clearance for your cargo, securing the release of the products, arranging delivery and transporting the goods to the importer warehouse and other functions.

It is not necessary for importers to employ a broker to enter goods on your behalf, however you will be required to put a Bond and deal with all administrative issues cited above.

Surety Bonds

Importers have to post a Bond with the Customs Service to ensure payment of the proper amount of taxes, duties and other associated charges for their cargo entry. The bonds are based on the value of the shipment and Customs determines the value of the required bond, some can be for one single entry and if you will be importing frequently it will be cheaper to get a continues bond to cover your import transactions for the year.

A surety bond company requires 100 percent collateral in the form of letter of credit or cashier's check and depends also on the financial condition of the importer. Usually the amount of the bond is three times the value of the shipment.

The Entry Process of Imports

When a legal commercial shipment reaches the ports of the United States it goes thru the following steps to be cleared:

- **Enters the designated port of entry**: Upon arrival of shipment at a U.S. pot of entry, the owner/agent must decide whether to enter the goods for consumption or place them into a bonded warehouse or free trade zone. The notification has to take place within 24 hours of landing in U.S. and documents of notification can be filed electronically.

- Documentation required includes evidence of right to make entry, commercial invoice or pro forma, packing list, evidence of bond.

- There are some especial permit for immediate delivery with alternative entry procedures that may provide you immediate release of shipment like in the case of importing fresh fruits and vegetables, goods for a trade fair, merchandise that is authorized by customs and specific cleared circumstances.

- **Valuation,** determines the value of the goods. The estimated duties or tariffs that have to paid by the importer. Customs value will be the transaction value or the price paid for merchandise when sold to the U.S.

- **Classification,** The responsibility rests with the importer, Custom Broker or the assigned person preparing the entry papers to get authorization and clearance. This classification of your cargo determines the ad valorem (percentage) tariff rate that will be applied to the valuation of the goods. You ought to consult the Tariff Schedule of the United States of America (TSUSA) and the Harmonized Tariff Schedule of the United States which will facilitate the import process.

- **Payment,** to obtain clearance all payments of duties must be made by check or cash to the Treasurer of the United States.

98

The Harmonized System

This is an international classification system designed to improve the collection of import and export duties and serve custom purposes in trade. It offers international uniformity in the presentation of customs tariffs and foreign trade statistics.

This Harmonized Tariff Schedule is referred to as HTSUS and is a large book that contains product classification employing a numbering system. There are over 5,000 article descriptions grouped in 21 sections and 97 chapters.

You may choose to purchase it you can for $99 as a book or CD from www.Boskage.com. It is also available and it can be downloaded from the International Trade Commission website at www.usitc.gov . All Custom Brokers have this valuable resource on their desk as they deal with multiple importers and hundreds of different products.

Import Quotas

The importation of certain products is controlled by quantity. As other countries do the U.S. also protects infant industries or established industries, for instance, textiles and apparel are subject to these quotas country by country and product by product.

The Customs Service maintains the status of these quotas and you can visit and consult the Journal of Commerce by accessing, www.customs.gov.

- *Absolute Quotas:* These are quantitative quotas. These quotas are a specified volume amount that is permitted for import during the quota period, year. Some quotas apply to certain countries and others can be global in nature. Once the quota is reached, the U.S. will not permit more imports of that product in stated time period.

- *Tariff-Rate Quotas:* These are imports for a specified quantity of a product that is taxed at a reduced rate of duty during a given rate. Other quantities entered above those established amounts are subject to higher duty rates.

Special U.S. Import Regulation and Notes

The U.S. allows for thousands of products to be imported, while many countries require an Import License to conduct imports, the U.S. does not.

While it is true that the U.S. is a large and highly regulated market as well as profitable and does not exist restrictions at large to import, certain classes of products or technology may be restricted or prohibited by other agencies to protect the economy and the security of the U.S., safeguarding the health or preserve domestic plants and animal life. Please visit the www.customs.gov import section.

The following are some of the agencies and commercial areas that if your product falls in their category, your product must abide and comply with their own regulations before importing.

- **Agricultural Commodities:** The U.S. Food and Drug Administration and the Department of Agriculture control and regulate the importation of animals, animal foods, plants, insects and poultry products.

- **Arms and Ammunition:** The Bureau of Alcohol, Tobacco and Firearms of the Department of the Treasure, prohibits the importation of these items except if it issues a license permit. Importation and Exportation of these products is prohibited unless license is issued by the Office of Munitions Control, Department of State in Washington D.C. You can visit, www.atf.treas.gov for more information.

- **Consumer Products:** The Consumer Product Safety Commission (CPSC) oversees safety issues relating to products such as refrigerators, freezers, dishwashers, television sets and other energy-using products. These products must meet safety and energy U.S. conservation standards.

- **Food, Drugs, Cosmetics and Medical Devices:** The Food and Drug Administration of the Department of Health and Human Services governs the importation of food, beverages, drugs, cosmetics and medical devices. There are strict guidelines from labeling products, to testing, clinical, certifications and compliance your product must meet before it is allowed for importation.

- **Textile, Wool and Fur Products:** Textile fiber products are required to be stamped, tagged and labeled as required by the Textile Fiber Products Identification Act and wool products must be in accordance with the Wool Products Labeling Act of 1939. Regulation can be obtained from the Federal Trade Commission, Washington, D.C.

- **Trademarks, Trade Names and Copyrights:** The Customs Reform and Simplification Act of 1979 enforced the protection of trademark owners against the importation of goods bearing counterfeit marks. Articles bearing trademarks or marks that copy or simulated a registered trademark of a United States or Foreign corporation is prohibited to be imported.

- **Wildlife and Pets:** The U.S. Fish and Wildlife Service of the Department of Interior in Washington, D.C. controls the importation of wild or game animals, birds and other wildlife, or any part or product made from those sources and the eggs of wild or game birds. The importation of birds, cats, dogs, monkeys and turtles and other animals is subject to the requirements of the U.S. Public Health Service, Center for Disease Control, Quarantine Division, Atlanta, Georgia.

101

Free Trade Zones and U.S. Foreign Trade Zones

Merchandise entering these free zones pay no tariff or taxes, under a guarantee bond that they will not enter the domestic market. If they are taken out from this zone, all duties must be paid, if they are approved to be cleared from Customs control. Typically in the Free Zones goods can be altered, stored, assembled and manufactured. These areas become areas that may circumvent barriers to free trade.

While around the world people know these are Free Zones, in the U.S. they are called Free Trade Zones (FTZ). Of course, these area are restricted and although located inside the territory under the supervision of the Customs Service, these area are considered outside the U.S.

These areas are located in or near customs ports of entry, industrial parks or warehouses. In these areas importers can bring merchandise to store, exhibit, assembled, manufactured or processed in some way. Quota restrictions are exempt from foreign merchandise control in these zones.

The U.S. government, see FTZs, as a way to stimulate international trade and contributing to the economic development of the region, creating jobs and income. The benefit to both importer and exporter accelerates business and commerce thus converting it to profits.

Customs Bonded Warehouse

This is an area, building or other secured area within the Customs territory where dutiable foreign merchandise may be stored for a period up to five years without payment of duty. As the importer you can be allowed to repacking, sorting or cleaning your merchandise but not removing anything unless you have been cleared by Customs.

The owner of the warehouse incurs the liability and must post a bond with the U.S. Customs Service and abide by the regulations and restrictions that pertain to the control and declaration of tariffs for goods on exiting the bonded warehouse area.

When importing in to U.S., I advice you as when exporting to become aware of the regulations and possibilities in the territory that are available to speed up trade. Likely, you might or not need to have the service of a Customs bonded warehouse or FTZ but plan and be aware of trade laws and the tools and resources available to win in the international trade.

CHAPTER 8

LATIN AMERICAN INFORMATION RESOURCES

Latin American Trade Associations in the United States

Argentina-American Chamber of Commerce

10 Rockefeller Plaza, Ste 1001
New York, NY 10020
Tel (212) 698-2238

Brazilian-American Chamber of Commerce

22 West 48th Street, Rm 404
Ney York, NY 10036
Tel (212) 575-9030

Brazilian-American Chamber of Commerce

80 Southwest Eight Street, Ste 1800
Miami, FL 33130
Tel (305) 579-9030

North American Chilean Chamber of Commerce

30 Vessey Street, Ste 506
New York, NY 10007
Tel (212) 233-7776

Colombian-American Chamber of Commerce

150 Nassau Street, Ste 2015
New York, NY 10038
Tel (212) 233-7776

Colombian-American Chamber of Commerce

250 Catalonia Avenue, Ste 407
Coral Gables, FL 33134
Tel (305) 446-2542

Ecuador-American Association

150 Nassau Street, Ste 2015
New York, NY 10038
Tel (212) 808-0978

Guatemala-U.S. Trade Association

299 Alhambra Circle, Ste 207
Coral Gables, FL 33134
Tel (305) 443-0343

Mexican Chamber of Commerce of Arizona

P.O. Box 626
Phoenix, AZ 85001
Tel (602) 252-6448

Mexican Chamber of Commerce of the Country of Los Angeles

125 Paseo de la Plaza, Room 404
Los Angeles, CA 90012
Tel (310) 826-9898

U.S.-Mexico Chamber of Commerce

1211 Connecticut Avenue N.W.
Washington, D.C. 20036
Tel (202) 296-5198

Peruvian-American Association

50 West 34th Street
New York, NY 10036

Trinidad and Tobago Chamber of Commerce

c/o Trintoc Services, Ltd.
400 Madison Avenue, Room 803
Ney York, NY 10016
Tel (212) 759-3388

Venezuela American Association of the United States

2332 Gallano Street
Coral Gables, FL 33134
Tel (305) 728-7042

Other U.S. Trade Associations

American Assoc. of Exporters and Importers

11 West 42nd Street
New York, NY 10036
Tel (212) 944-2230

Chamber of Commerce of the United States

International Division
1615 H Street N.W.
Washington, D.C. 20062
Tel (202) 463-5460

Council of the Americas

680 Park Avenue
New York, NY 10021
Tel (212) 628-3200

Federation of International Trade Associations

1900 Campus Commons Drive, Ste 340
Reston, VA 20191
Tel (703) 620-1588

Houston Inter-American Chamber of Commerce

510 Bering Drive, Ste 300
Houston, TX 77057
Tel (713) 975-6171

Latin American Chamber of Commerce

3512 Fullerton Ave
Chicago, IL 60647
Tel (773) 252-5211

Latin American Manufacturers Association

419 New Jersey Avenue S.E.
Washington, D.C. 20003
Tel (202) 546-3803

National Customs Brokers & Forwarders Association of America

1200 18th Street N.W., Ste 901
Washington, D.C. 20036
Tel (202) 466-0222

NEXCO (formerly National Association of Export Companies)

P.O. Box 3949
Grand Central Station
New York, NY 10163
Tel (877) 29-4901

Pan American Society of the United States

680 Park Avenues
New York, NY 10021
Tel (212) 249-8950

Small Business Exports Association

1156 15th Street N.W., Suite 1100
Washington, D.C. 20005
Tel (202) 659-9320

United States Council for International Business

1212 Avenue of the Americas
New York, NY 10036
Tel (212) 354-4480

U.S. Hispanic Chamber of Commerce

1030 15th Street N.W., Ste 206
Washington, D.C. 20005
Tel (202) 842-1212

World Trade Centers Association

60 East 4nd Street, Ste 1901
New York, NY 10165
Tel (212) 432-26226

CPSIA information can be obtained
at www.ICGtesting.com
Printed in the USA
LVOW04s1506030816
498915LV00019B/1258/P